Show me

Excel 4
A Visual Guide to the Basics

Clayton Walnum

alpha books

A Division of Prentice Hall Computer Publishing
11711 North College Avenue, Carmel, Indiana 46032 USA

To Stu, but this time from farther away.

©1993 Alpha Books

All rights reserved. No part of this book shall be reproduced, stored in a retrieval system, or transmitted by any means, electronic, mechanical, photocopying, recording, or otherwise, without written permission from the publisher. No patent liability is assumed with respect to the use of the information contained herein. Although every precaution has been taken in the preparation of this book, the publisher and author assume no responsibility for errors or omissions. Neither is any liability assumed for damages resulting from the use of the information contained herein. For information, address Alpha Books, 11711 North College Avenue, Carmel, IN 46032.

International Standard Book Number: 93-70254
Library of Congress Catalog Card Number: 1-56761-179-6

95 94 93   8 7 6 5 4 3 2 1

Interpretation of the printing code: the rightmost number of the first series of numbers is the year of the book's printing; the rightmost number of the second series of numbers is the number of the book's printing. For example, a printing code of 93-1 shows that the first printing of the book occurred in 1993.

Screen reproductions in this book were created by means of the program Collage Plus from Inner Media, Inc., Hollis, NH.

Printed in the United States of America

TRADEMARKS

All terms mentioned in this book that are known to be trademarks have been appropriately capitalized. Alpha Books cannot attest to the accuracy of this information. Use of a term in this book should not be regarded as affecting the validity of any trademark or service mark.

Publisher: Marie Butler-Knight
Associate Publisher: Lisa A. Bucki
Managing Editor: Elizabeth Keaffaber
Acquisitions Manager: Stephen R. Poland
Development Editor: Faithe Wempen
Manuscript Editor: San Dee Phillips
Cover Designer: Scott Fullmer
Designer: Roger Morgan
Indexer: Jeanne Clark
Production Team: Diana Bigham, Tim Cox, Linda Koopman, Tom Loveman, Beth Rago, Greg Simsic

Special thanks to C. Herbert Feltner for ensuring the technical accuracy of this book.

CONTENTS

	Introduction	1
Part 1	Beginning Excel Tasks	11

Starting Excel 12
Choosing Menu Commands 14
Controlling Excel's Windows 17
Working with Dialog Boxes 20
Using Toolbars and Toolboxes 22
Getting Help 24
Opening an Existing Worksheet 27
Opening a New Worksheet 29
Closing a Worksheet 30
Saving a Worksheet 32
Saving a Worksheet with a Different Name 33
Deleting a Worksheet 35
Quitting Excel 36

Part 2	Building a Worksheet	37

Selecting Cells 38
Entering Labels 40
Entering Values 42
Entering Dates and Times 44
Entering Formulas 46
Using Cell References in Formulas 49
Using Cell Ranges in Formulas 51
Using Excel's Built-In Functions 52

Part 3	Editing and Formatting a Worksheet	55

Editing Cell Contents 56
Moving and Copying Cells 58
Inserting Rows and Columns 61
Deleting Rows and Columns 63
Clearing Cells 65

iii

Finding Data in Cells...67
Replacing Data in Cells 68
Sorting Data 69
Changing Number Formats......................................72
Aligning Data in Cells...73
Changing Cell Widths 75
Changing Fonts and Text Attributes........................77

Part 4 Charting Data in a Worksheet   79

Creating a Chart with ChartWizard..........................80
Changing a Chart's Type 84
Giving a Chart Its Own Window 86
Editing a Chart with ChartWizard............................88
Changing Values on a Chart 90
Adding a Chart Legend 92
Deleting Chart Elements...94
Clearing a DataSeries or Format 95
Deleting an Embedded Chart 96

Part 5 Printing a Worksheet   97

Selecting a Printer 98
Printing an Entire Worksheet...................................99
Printing Part of a Worksheet 101
Using Print Preview 103
Setting Up Pages...105
Using Page Breaks 107
Printing Row or Column Titles 110
Adding Headers and Footers 112

Installing Excel   115

Glossary   119

Index   123

INTRODUCTION

Have you ever said to yourself, "I wish someone would just *show me* how to use Microsoft Excel?" If you have, this Show Me book is for you. In it, you won't find detailed explanations of what's going on in your computer each time you enter a command. Instead, you will see pictures that show you, step-by-step, how to perform a particular task.

This book will make you feel as though you have your very own personal trainer standing next to you, pointing at the screen, and showing you exactly what to do.

WHAT IS EXCEL?

Excel is a spreadsheet program. Using Excel, you can create, manipulate, and analyze complex collections of data. These data collections are called spreadsheets.

Using Excel, you can easily:

- Create tables of data.
- Use formulas to calculate new information from your data.
- Produce colorful charts based on your data.
- Print out as many copies of a spreadsheet as you want.
- Save your work so that next month you can change a spreadsheet without having to recreate it.

LEARNING THE LINGO

Spreadsheet: A collection of data organized into rows and columns and displayed on your computer's screen.

Spreadsheet program: A program such as Excel used to create spreadsheets and to manipulate the spreadsheet's data in various ways in order to produce tables, charts, and reports.

A Day in the Life of a Spreadsheet

What you create with Excel is called a document. So, whether you use Excel to create a spreadsheet, a report, or a chart, you are creating individual documents. You can save documents, print documents, and edit (change) documents. As you create your document in Excel, you'll follow a basic pattern:

Open an existing document, or create a new one. You start your work session by typing data into a new document or by editing an existing one.

Type in some data. This part is easy; just type!

Review what you've typed and make changes. At this stage, you're copying or moving data from one place to another. You may even delete some data or insert new data to refine a table. The process of making changes to existing data is called editing.

Add pizzazz. Changing the way data looks (such as adding bold or making characters bigger) is called formatting.

Save your document. Once you're sure you have a document that you like, you should save it. Actually, it's best to save a document often during the editing phase so you can't lose any changes.

View your document before you print it. Excel gives you several ways to view your data, as you are working and right before you print your document.

Print your document. Nothing is better than holding the finished product in your own hands.

The Odds and Ends of Using a Spreadsheet Program

Before you can use Excel, you need to understand a few simple terms. First, a spreadsheet (or a "worksheet" as it's called in the Excel manuals) is comprised of many *cells* organized into rows and columns. Each cell can hold a single piece of *data*. "Data" is just a fancy computer word for information. In Excel's case, the data in a cell is usually a *value*, *text*, or a *formula*.

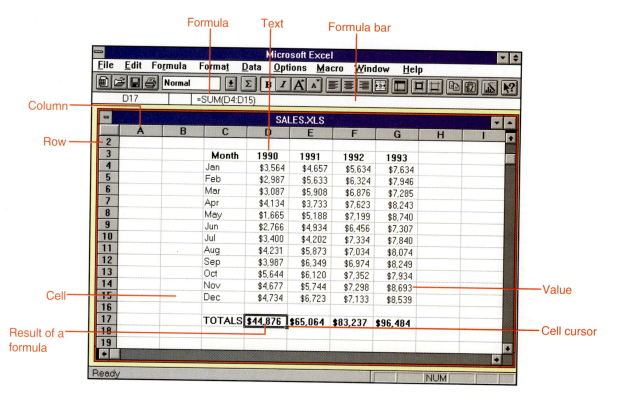

While values and text appear in a cell just as you type them, a formula appears only in the formula bar. As you can see in the figure, a cell that contains a formula shows the result of the formula. In the figure, the bottom row of cells contains four formulas, each of which sums the values in its column.

The *cell cursor* marks the place where data will be inserted. To insert data into a spreadsheet, you move the cell cursor (a black box) to the cell where you want the data stored, and then you type.

Formatting in a spreadsheet describes how data looks. Character formatting describes how a character looks. (For example, is it bold or italic?) Number formatting describes the way values appear on the screen. (For example, is the value currency?)

LEARNING THE LINGO

Data: Information in a computer.

Cell: The smallest part of a spreadsheet. Each cell holds a single piece of data.

Cell cursor: A black box that appears on the currently selected cell.

Formatting: The process of changing the look of a character (for example, by making it bold, underlined, and slightly bigger) or a value (for example, by adding a dollar sign or a decimal point).

Value: A number that you type into a cell.

Text: Characters that cannot be used in calculations.

Formula: Symbols and characters that calculate new values.

Cell References

In order to create formulas, you need some way to refer to cells that contain values. In Excel, as in most spreadsheet programs, you refer to a cell by typing its column letter and row number. In the figure above, for example, cell **C4** contains the text **Jan**, whereas cell **D15** contains the value **$4,734**.

Often, you need to refer to a block of cells in a formula. You can do this easily by first typing the name of the cell in the upper left corner of the block, followed by a colon (:) and the name of the cell in the lower right corner of the block. For example, to refer to all the values in the table shown in the figure, you would type **D4:G15**.

As you work with Excel, you will need to use many cell references, so it's important that you understand how to create them.

HOW TO USE THIS BOOK

Using this book is as simple as falling off your chair. Just flip to the task that you want to perform and follow the steps. You will see easy step-by-step instructions that tell you which keys to press and which commands to select. You will also see step-by-step pictures that show you what to do. Follow the steps or the pictures (or both) to complete the task.

Opening a New Document

1 Click on the File menu, or press **Alt+F**.

2 Click on New, or press **N**.

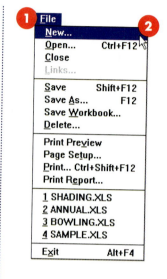

3 Select **Worksheet**.

4 Click on **OK**, or press **Enter**.

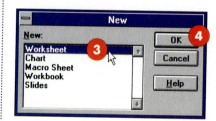

Every computer book has its own way of telling you which buttons to push and which keys to press. Here's how this book handles those formalities:

- Keys that you should press appear as they do on your keyboard; for example, press **Alt** or press **F10**. If you need to press more than one key at once, the keys are separated with plus signs. For example, if the text tells you to press **Alt+F**, hold down the **Alt** key while pressing the **F** key.

- Text that you should type is printed in **boldface type like this.**

- Some commands are activated by selecting a menu and then a command. If I tell you to "select **F**ile **N**ew," you should open the **F**ile menu and select the **N**ew command. In this book, the selection letter is printed in boldface for easy recognition.

LEARNING THE LINGO

Selection letter: A single letter of a menu command, such as the **x** in E**x**it, which activates the command when the menu is open and that letter is pressed.

Definitions in Plain English

In addition to the basic step-by-step approach, pages may contain Learn the Lingo definitions to help you understand key terms. These definitions are placed off to the side, so you can easily skip them.

LEARNING THE LINGO

Pull-down menu: A menu that appears at the top of the screen, listing various options. The menu is not visible until you select it from the menu bar. The menu then drops down, covering a small part of the screen.

Quick Refreshers

If you need to know how to perform some other task in order to perform the current task, look for a Quick Refresher. With the Quick Refresher, you won't have to flip through the book to learn how to perform the other task; the information is right where you need it.

QUICK REFRESHER

Making dialog box selections

List box: Click on a list item to choose it. Use the scrollbar to view additional items.

Drop-down list: Click on the down arrow to the right of the list to display it. Click on the desired item.

Text box: Click to place the I-beam in the box. Type your entry.

Check box: Click on a box to select or deselect it. (You can select more than one.)

Option button: Click on a button to select it. (You can select only one button in a group.)

Command button: Click on a button to execute the command. (All dialog boxes have at least two command buttons: OK to execute your selections, and Cancel to cancel the selections.)

Tips, Ideas, and Shortcuts

Throughout this book, you will encounter tips that provide important information about a task or tell you how to perform the task more quickly.

Exercises

Because most people learn by doing, exercises throughout the book give you additional practice performing a task.

Exercise

TIP

Here are some keyboard shortcuts for opening and saving files and for exiting the program:

Open File   CTRL + F10

Save File   SHIFT + F12

Exit   ALT + F4

Practice what you've learned about using menus by closing the open document.

1. Open the **File** menu by clicking on it or by pressing **Alt+F**.

2. Select **Close** by clicking on it or by pressing **C**.

3. If you're asked to save your changes, click on **No** or press **N**. (We haven't done anything worth saving yet.)

Where Should You Start?

If this is your first encounter with computers, read the next section, "Quick Computer Tour" before reading anything else. This section explains some computer basics that you need to know in order to get your computer up and running.

Once you know the basics, you can work through this book from beginning to end or skip around from task to task, as needed. If you decide to skip around, there are several ways you can find what you're looking for:

- Use the Table of Contents at the front of this book to find a specific task you want to perform.

- Use the complete index at the back of this book to look up a specific task or topic and find the page number on which it is covered.

- Use the color coded sections to find groups of related tasks.

- Flip through the book, and look at the task titles at the top of the pages. This method works best if you know the general location of the task in the book.
- Use the inside back cover of this book to quickly find the page where a command you are looking for is covered.

QUICK COMPUTER TOUR

If this is your first time in front of a computer, the next few sections will teach you the least you need to know to get started.

Parts of a Computer

Think of a computer as a car. The system unit holds the engine that powers the computer. The monitor is like the windshield that lets you see where you're going. And the keyboard and mouse are like the steering wheel, which allow you to control the computer.

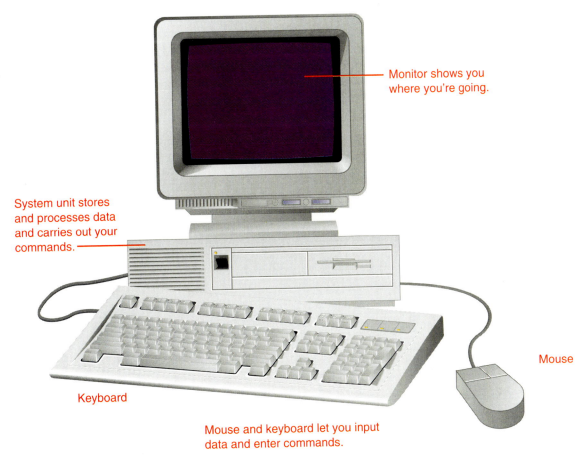

Monitor shows you where you're going.

System unit stores and processes data and carries out your commands.

Mouse

Keyboard

Mouse and keyboard let you input data and enter commands.

The System Unit

The system unit contains three basic elements: a central processing unit (CPU) that does all the "thinking" for the computer; random-access memory (RAM) that stores instructions and data while the CPU is processing it; and disk drives, which store information permanently on disks to keep the information safe. It also contains several ports (at the back), which allow you to connect other devices to it, such as a keyboard, mouse, and printer.

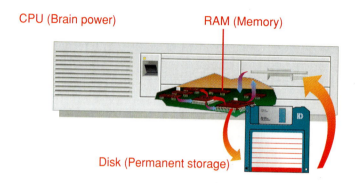

Using a Keyboard

The keyboard is no mystery. It contains a set of alphanumeric (letter and number) keys for entering text, arrow keys for moving around on-screen, and function keys (F1, F2, and so on) for entering commands. It also has some odd keys, including Alt (Alternative), Ctrl (Control), and Esc (Escape) that perform special actions.

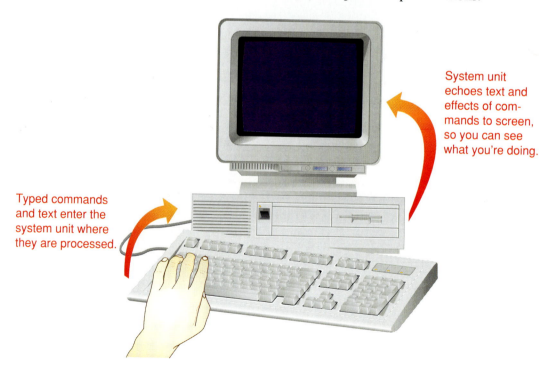

8

Using a Mouse

Like the keyboard, a mouse allows you to communicate with the computer. You roll the mouse around on your desk to move a mouse pointer on the screen. You can use the pointer to open menus and select other items on-screen. Here are some mouse techniques you must master:

- *Pointing.* To point, roll the mouse on your desk until the tip of the mouse pointer is on the item you want to point to.

- *Clicking.* To click on an item, point to the desired item, and then hold the mouse steady while you press and release the mouse button. Use the left mouse button unless I tell you specifically to use the right button.

- *Double-clicking.* To double-click, hold the mouse steady while you press and release the mouse button twice quickly.

- *Right-clicking.* To right-click, click using the right mouse button instead of the left button.

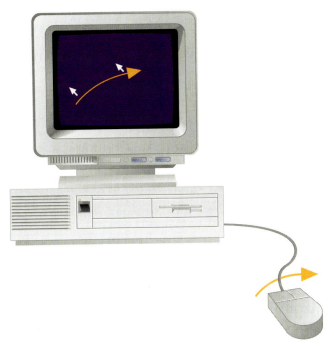

Understanding Disks, Directories, and Files

Whatever you type (a letter, a list of names, a tax return) is stored only in your computer's temporary memory and is erased when the electricity is turned off. To protect your work, you must save it in a file on a disk.

A file is like a folder that you might use to store a report or a letter. You name the file, so you can later find and retrieve the information it contains.

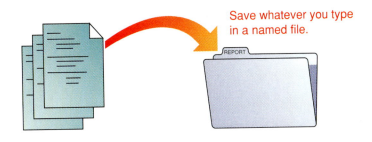

Save whatever you type in a named file.

Files are stored on disks. Your computer probably has a hard disk inside it (called drive C) to which you can save your files. You can also save files to floppy disks, which you insert into the slots (the floppy disk drives) on the front of the computer.

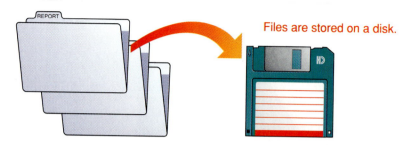

Files are stored on a disk.

To keep files organized on a disk, you can create directories on the disk. Each directory acts as a drawer in a filing cabinet, storing a group of related files. Although you can create directories on both floppy and hard disks, most people use directories only on hard disks.

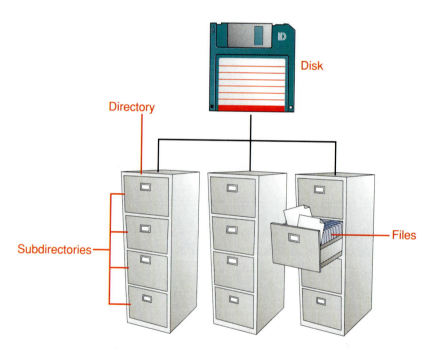

PART 1

Beginning Excel Tasks

This part describes basic Excel tasks that you need to know to get started. When you have finished this part, you will be able to start Excel, manipulate Excel's menus and dialog boxes, manage worksheets, get help, and quit Excel.

- Starting Excel
- Choosing Menu Commands
- Controlling Excel's Windows
- Working with Dialog Boxes
- Using Toolbars and Toolboxes
- Getting Help
- Opening an Existing Worksheet
- Opening a New Worksheet
- Closing a Worksheet
- Saving a Worksheet
- Saving a Worksheet with a Different Name
- Deleting a Worksheet
- Quitting Excel

STARTING EXCEL

Why Start Excel?

You must start Excel before you can use it. When you start Excel, the program loads into your computer's memory, and a main window appears. From this main window, you control the program, creating worksheets, charts, and other documents. Excel must be started from within Windows; if Windows is not running, type **WIN** at the DOS prompt to start it.

> **TIP**
>
> Before you can start Excel, it must be installed on your computer. To install Excel, refer to "Installing Microsoft Excel" in *User's Guide 1*, one of the manuals that came with Excel, or refer to this book's Appendix A.

Starting Excel

1 Turn on your computer.

2 At the DOS prompt, type **WIN** and press **Enter**.

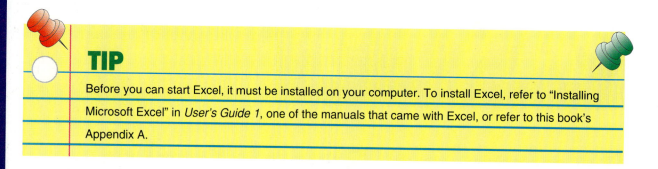

3 If the Microsoft Excel 4.0 group window is minimized, double-click on its **program group icon**.

You can also select the Excel window from the Window menu.

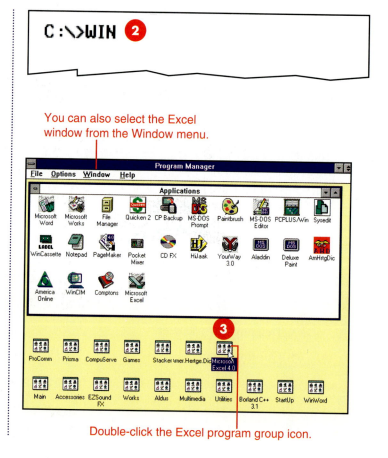

Double-click the Excel program group icon.

STARTING EXCEL

 Double-click on the **Microsoft Excel** icon.

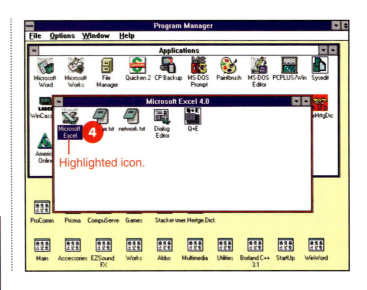

Highlighted icon.

LEARNING THE LINGO

Point: Position the mouse pointer over an object on the screen.

Click: Press and release the left mouse button.

Double-click: Press and release the left mouse button twice quickly.

Program icon: A small picture representing a program you can run. The program name usually appears under the picture.

Program group: A window containing one or more program icons.

Program group icon: A small picture representing a program group that has been minimized.

Minimized: Shrunken to the size of an icon; windows that are not in use are often minimized so they do not clutter the screen.

TIP

If Windows is new to you, you may not be familiar with program groups and icons.

A *program group icon* represents a minimized program group. When you double-click it, a program group icon opens into a program group.

A *program icon* represents a program you can run. When you double-click it, the program runs.

TIP

Windows applications like Excel are designed to be easily controlled by a mouse. If you don't have a mouse, you should seriously consider adding one to your system. This book assumes that you have a mouse.

13

CHOOSING MENU COMMANDS

What Are Menu Commands?

All the commands needed to control Excel are located in the menus on the main menu bar. You can use your mouse or your keyboard to select any menu or menu command. When you open a menu, you'll see that they often contain check marks, ellipses, and grayed-out commands. These and other menu elements are explained below:

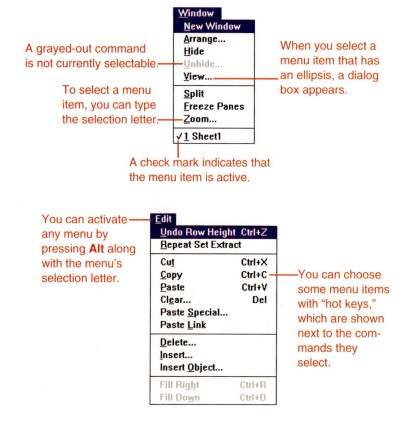

LEARNING THE LINGO

Hot Keys: Keystrokes you can use to instantly select a menu command.

Grayed-out: Grayed-out menu commands are displayed lighter than other commands and cannot be selected.

Ellipsis: An ellipsis is three dots (...). When an ellipsis follows a menu command, the command displays a dialog box when selected.

Check marks: A check mark next to a menu option means the option is currently selected.

Selection letter: The underlined letter in a menu or command menu.

CHOOSING MENU COMMANDS

Choosing Menu Commands

1 Click on the menu name on the menu bar, or hold down the **Alt** key and type the selection letter in the menu name.

2 Click on the menu command you want, or type the selection letter in the command name.

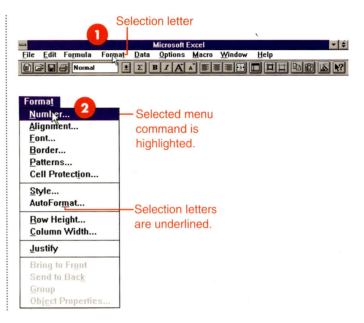

Selection letter

Selected menu command is highlighted.

Selection letters are underlined.

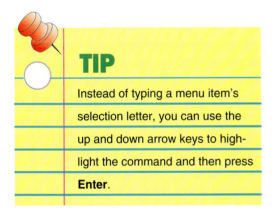

TIP

Instead of typing a menu item's selection letter, you can use the up and down arrow keys to highlight the command and then press **Enter**.

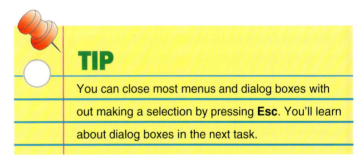

TIP

You can close most menus and dialog boxes without making a selection by pressing **Esc**. You'll learn about dialog boxes in the next task.

Beginning Excel Tasks

CHOOSING MENU COMMANDS

Exercise

Practice selecting menu commands by choosing the **D**isplay command on the **O**ptions menu, which opens the Display Options dialog box.

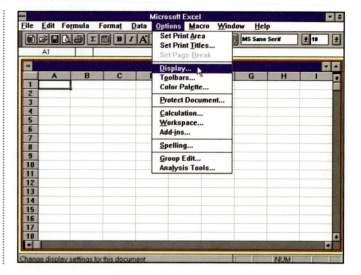

1 Click on the **O**ptions menu, or press **Alt+O**.

2 Click on **D**isplay, or press **D**.

3 Press **Esc** to clear the dialog box from your screen.

TIP

If you open a menu by pressing **Alt** along with the menu's selection (underlined) letter, you can then view other menus in the menu bar by pressing your left or right arrow keys.

16

CONTROLLING EXCEL'S WINDOWS

Why Control Windows?

Excel's windows contain many controls that you can use to manipulate the window or its contents. Using these controls, you can change the size of a window, move it around the screen, change its contents, close it, and more.

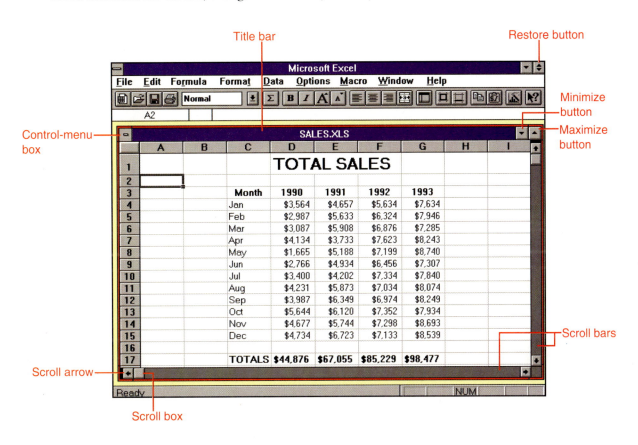

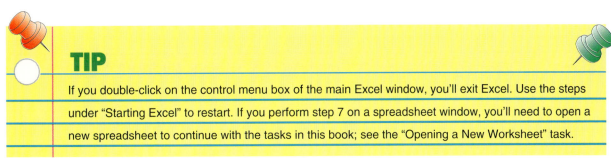

TIP

If you double-click on the control menu box of the main Excel window, you'll exit Excel. Use the steps under "Starting Excel" to restart. If you perform step 7 on a spreadsheet window, you'll need to open a new spreadsheet to continue with the tasks in this book; see the "Opening a New Worksheet" task.

CONTROLLING EXCEL'S WINDOWS

Controlling a Window

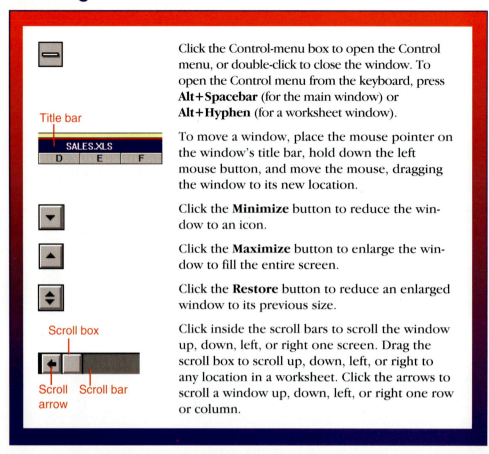

Click the Control-menu box to open the Control menu, or double-click to close the window. To open the Control menu from the keyboard, press **Alt+Spacebar** (for the main window) or **Alt+Hyphen** (for a worksheet window).

To move a window, place the mouse pointer on the window's title bar, hold down the left mouse button, and move the mouse, dragging the window to its new location.

Click the **Minimize** button to reduce the window to an icon.

Click the **Maximize** button to enlarge the window to fill the entire screen.

Click the **Restore** button to reduce an enlarged window to its previous size.

Click inside the scroll bars to scroll the window up, down, left, or right one screen. Drag the scroll box to scroll up, down, left, or right to any location in a worksheet. Click the arrows to scroll a window up, down, left, or right one row or column.

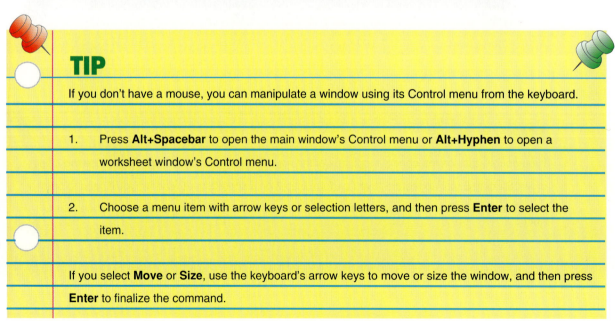

TIP

If you don't have a mouse, you can manipulate a window using its Control menu from the keyboard.

1. Press **Alt+Spacebar** to open the main window's Control menu or **Alt+Hyphen** to open a worksheet window's Control menu.

2. Choose a menu item with arrow keys or selection letters, and then press **Enter** to select the item.

If you select **Move** or **Size**, use the keyboard's arrow keys to move or size the window, and then press **Enter** to finalize the command.

CONTROLLING EXCEL'S WINDOWS

Exercise

In this exercise, you'll use the various controls to manipulate an Excel worksheet window.

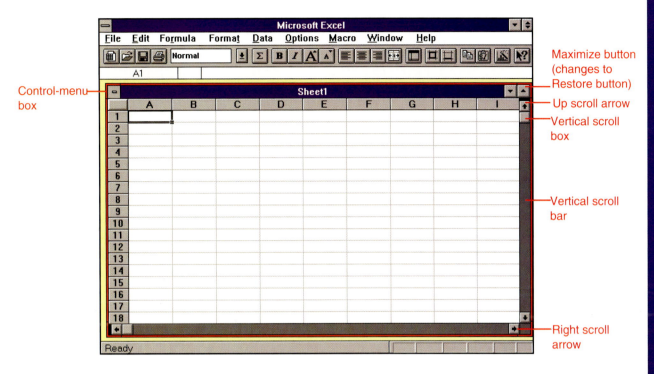

1. Click below the scroll box on the vertical scroll bar to scroll the window down one screen.

2. Click to the right of the scroll box on the horizontal scroll bar to scroll the window to the right one screen.

3. Click on the up scroll arrow to scroll the window up one row.

4. Click on the right scroll arrow to scroll the window right one column.

5. Click the maximize button to enlarge the window to the full screen.

6. Click the restore button (the lower one) to reduce the window to its original size.

7. Double-click the Control-menu box to close the window.

WORKING WITH DIALOG BOXES

What Are Dialog Boxes?

Dialog boxes appear when you issue certain commands. They are small windows containing various controls and text fields with which you can provide information to Excel. Sometimes a dialog box displays only a simple question; other times a dialog box contains many lists, buttons, text-entry fields, and other controls.

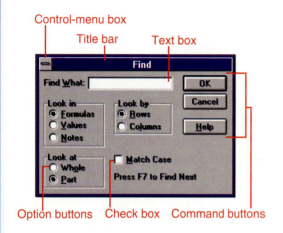

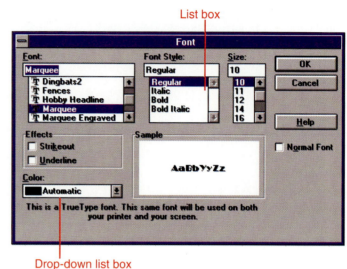

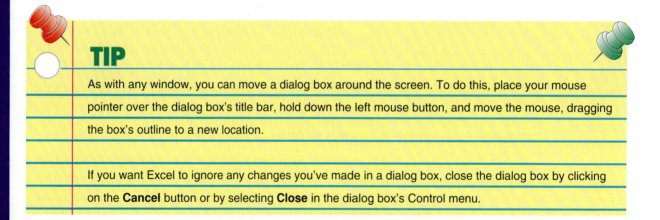

TIP

As with any window, you can move a dialog box around the screen. To do this, place your mouse pointer over the dialog box's title bar, hold down the left mouse button, and move the mouse, dragging the box's outline to a new location.

If you want Excel to ignore any changes you've made in a dialog box, close the dialog box by clicking on the **Cancel** button or by selecting **Close** in the dialog box's Control menu.

LEARNING THE LINGO

Toggle: To switch an option from on to off or from off to on.

Drag: Point to a screen object and then hold down the left mouse button while you move the mouse, dragging the pointer across the screen.

WORKING WITH DIALOG BOXES

Selecting Dialog Box Options

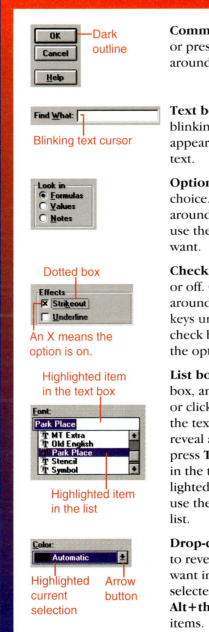

Dark outline

Blinking text cursor

Dotted box

An X means the option is on.

Highlighted item in the text box

Highlighted item in the list

Highlighted current selection

Arrow button

Command buttons: Click the button you want, or press **Tab** until a dark outline appears around the button, and then press **Enter**.

Text boxes: Click the text box to activate the blinking text cursor, or press **Tab** until it appears in the text box. Then type the required text.

Option buttons: Click on the button of your choice. Or press **Tab** until a dotted box appears around the currently selected option, and then use the arrow keys to move to the option you want.

Check boxes: Click on an option to turn it on or off. Or press **Tab** until a dotted box appears around an option in that area; use the arrow keys until the dotted box moves to the desired check box; and then press the **Spacebar** to turn the option on or off.

List boxes: Click on the text box above the list box, and then type the item you want to select, or click on an item from the list to place it in the text box. Use the scroll bar, if needed, to reveal additional choices. Or with the keyboard, press **Tab** until the blinking text cursor appears in the text box or its current contents is highlighted. Then either type the item you want or use the arrow keys to highlight an item in the list.

Drop-down list box: Click on the arrow button to reveal the list, and then click on the item you want in the list. Or press **Tab** until the currently selected item is highlighted, and then press **Alt+the arrow keys** to display the available items.

21

USING TOOLBARS AND TOOLBOXES

Why Use Toolbars and Toolboxes?

Many frequently used commands appear on Excel's Toolbar, where they can be selected with a quick click of your mouse. Using the Toolbar can save you from having to open a lot of menus.

To help with some special tasks, such as formatting charts, you can open additional Toolbars or Toolboxes. Toolboxes differ from Toolbars in that you can move them around the screen, placing them wherever they're convenient.

Selecting Commands from a Toolbar or Toolbox

To select a command from a Toolbar or Toolbox, place your mouse pointer over the command's button and click.

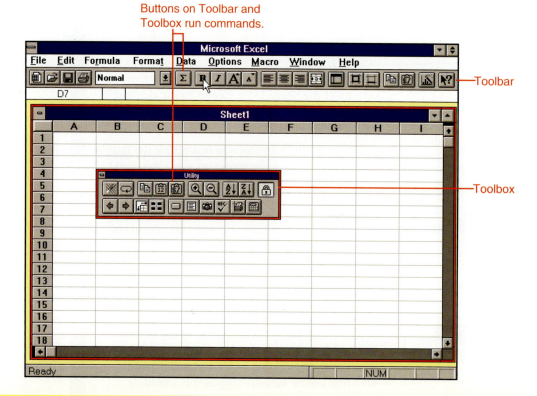

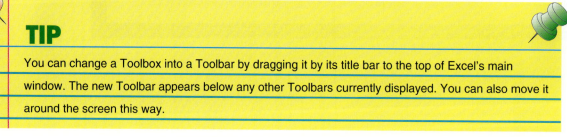

TIP

You can change a Toolbox into a Toolbar by dragging it by its title bar to the top of Excel's main window. The new Toolbar appears below any other Toolbars currently displayed. You can also move it around the screen this way.

USING TOOLBARS AND TOOLBOXES

Opening a Toolbar or Toolbox

1 Select Toolbars from the Options menu.

2 Select the name of the Toolbar you want to open.

3 Select the Show button.

TIP

If you're not sure what a particular command button does, place your mouse pointer over the command button and hold down the left mouse button. A description of the command appears at the bottom of Excel's window. If you decide not to select the command, keep the left mouse button down until you move the mouse pointer off the command button.

LEARNING THE LINGO

Command button: An on-screen button object that you can click to select a specific Excel command.

Toolbar: A stationary row of command buttons at the top or bottom of Excel's main window.

Toolbox: A small, movable box containing command buttons.

23

GETTING HELP

Why Use On-line Help?

Because Excel is a complicated program containing hundreds of commands, Microsoft added a comprehensive on-line help system, so you can find answers to your questions quickly. Access Excel's help system from the **Help** menu or by simply pressing **F1**.

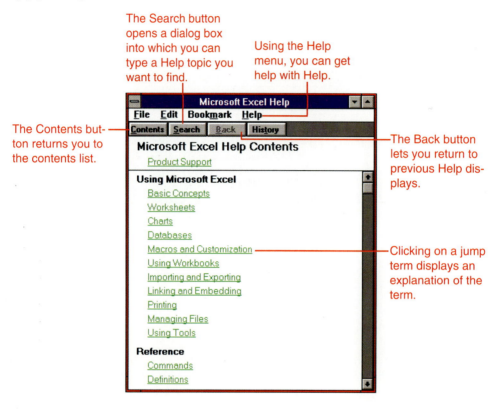

The Search button opens a dialog box into which you can type a Help topic you want to find.

Using the Help menu, you can get help with Help.

The Contents button returns you to the contents list.

The Back button lets you return to previous Help displays.

Clicking on a jump term displays an explanation of the term.

Getting Help on a Specific Topic

1 Select **Contents** from the **Help** menu.

2 Select **Search**.

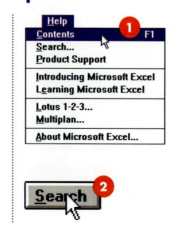

24

GETTING HELP

3 Type the topic for which you need help, and press **Enter**.

4 Select a topic from the list at the bottom of the dialog box.

5 Select **G**o To.

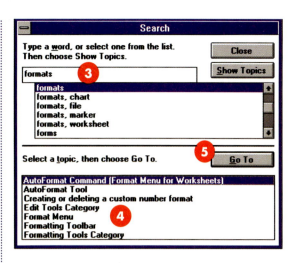

6 Read the **H**elp text for the topic, using the scroll bar or the **PgDn** and **PgUp** keys to scroll the text.

7 Click on any jump terms you want to read about.

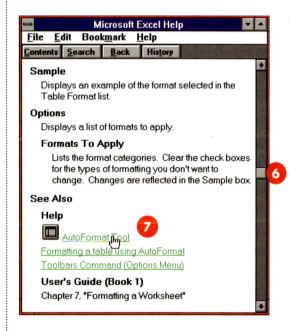

8 Double-click the Help window's Control box to close **H**elp, or click once on it and select **C**lose.

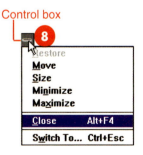

25

GETTING HELP

Exercise

To get some practice with Help, use it to find information on Excel's formatting toolbar.

1 Select **Search** from the Help menu.

2 Type **Toolbars**, and press **Enter**.

3 Select **Formatting Toolbar** at the bottom of the dialog box.

4 Select **Go** To.

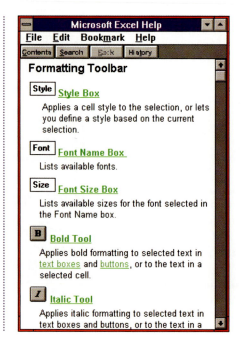

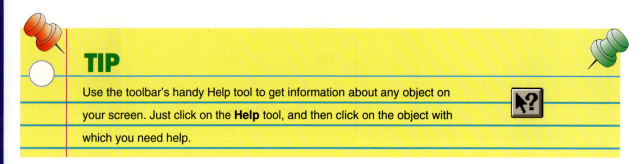

TIP

Use the toolbar's handy Help tool to get information about any object on your screen. Just click on the **Help** tool, and then click on the object with which you need help.

26

OPENING AN EXISTING WORKSHEET

Why Open an Existing Worksheet?

When Excel first appears on your screen, it opens a blank worksheet window called **Sheet1**.

If you're starting a new worksheet, you can use this default worksheet. However, often you'll want to open a worksheet that you previously created and saved to your hard disk. To open an existing spreadsheet, select **O**pen from the **F**ile menu.

Opening an Existing Worksheet

1 Select **O**pen from the **F**ile menu, or press **Ctrl+F12**.

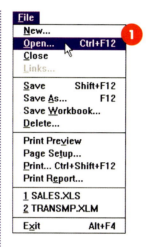

2 Double-click the directory that contains the file, or highlight it and press **Enter**.

3 Double-click the file, or highlight it and select **OK**.

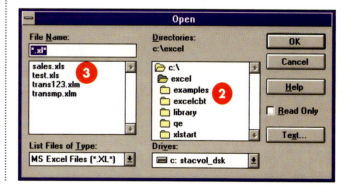

Beginning Excel Tasks

OPENING AN EXISTING WORKSHEET

Exercise

In this exercise, you'll open the file **BILL1.XLT**, which you'll find in Excel's **EXAMPLES** directory.

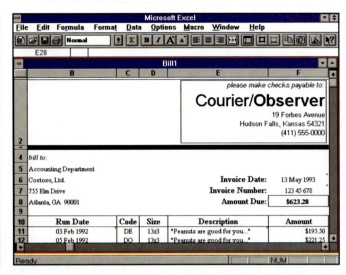

1 Select **O**pen from the **F**ile menu, or press **Ctrl+F12**.

2 Select the **EXAMPLES** directory, and then press **Enter**. Or double-click on the **EXAMPLES** directory.

3 Select **BILL1.XLT**, and then select **OK**, or press **Enter**.

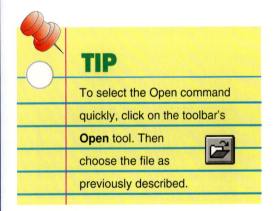

TIP

To select the Open command quickly, click on the toolbar's **Open** tool. Then choose the file as previously described.

QUICK REFRESHER

To use a list box from the keyboard, press **Tab** until the blinking text cursor appears in the text box or until the currently selected item in the text box is highlighted. (When the item in the text box contains wild card characters, such as asterisks, as it does in the File Name text box, you must press **Tab** once more to make a dotted box appear in the list box.) Then use the up or down arrow keys to highlight the item in the list.

LEARNING THE LINGO

File: Your worksheets are stored on your hard disk in a *file*, a collection of related data stored as a single unit.

Directory: Directories are like little file cabinets on your hard drive that help you organize your files. They can contain either files or other directories.

OPENING A NEW WORKSHEET

Why Open a New Worksheet?

If you've already used Sheet1 and want to start yet another worksheet, you can do it by selecting **New** from the **File** menu.

Opening a New Worksheet

1. Select **New** from the **File** menu.
2. Select **Worksheet**.
3. Select **OK**.

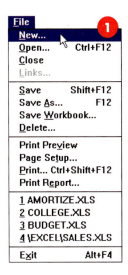

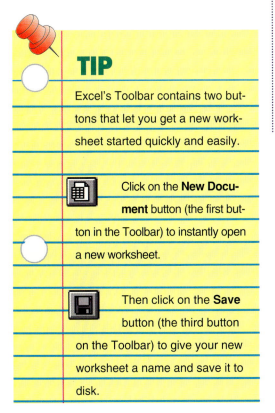

TIP

Excel's Toolbar contains two buttons that let you get a new worksheet started quickly and easily.

Click on the **New Document** button (the first button in the Toolbar) to instantly open a new worksheet.

Then click on the **Save** button (the third button on the Toolbar) to give your new worksheet a name and save it to disk.

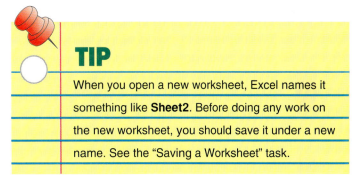

TIP

When you open a new worksheet, Excel names it something like **Sheet2**. Before doing any work on the new worksheet, you should save it under a new name. See the "Saving a Worksheet" task.

29

CLOSING A WORKSHEET

Why Close a Worksheet?

After you're finished viewing a worksheet, you may want to close it, which removes the worksheet from your screen and from your computer's memory. (The worksheet still exists on your disk, however, so you can open it again any time you like.) By closing worksheets you no longer currently need, you'll have fewer Excel windows to manage. You'll also give Excel more memory with which to work.

TIP

If you make changes to a worksheet—changes you want to keep—you must save the worksheet before closing it. Refer to the "Saving a Worksheet" task.

TIP

Here are two alternative ways to close a document: open the **File** menu, and select **C**lose; or click on the window's Control-menu box to open the Control menu, and then select **C**lose.

LEARNING THE LINGO

Active window: The *active* window, which is the only window you can work on, is the window on top of any other open windows. If you have only one window open, that window is always active.

Inactive window: *Inactive* windows are any windows other than the active window that are currently open. Inactive windows are always partially covered by other windows.

CLOSING A WORKSHEET

Closing a Worksheet

1 Open the **W**indow menu, and select the worksheet you want to close.

2 Double-click the window's Control-menu box, or press **Ctrl+F4**.

TIP

If you make changes to a worksheet and then try to close it, Excel asks if you want to save your changes. Select **Y**es to save the changes, select **N**o to close the worksheet without saving the changes, or select **Cancel** to cancel the Close command.

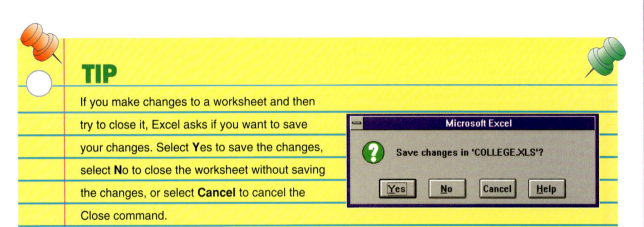

SAVING A WORKSHEET

Why Save a Worksheet?

When you exit Excel, all the worksheets currently open are removed from memory. If you haven't saved any changes, there's no way to get them back. You must save your worksheets to disk so that they will be available to view or edit later. Select **S**ave from the **F**ile menu to save your worksheets.

Saving a Worksheet

1 If you have more than one worksheet open, choose the worksheet you want to save from the **W**indow menu, or click anywhere within the window.

2 Select **S**ave from the **F**ile menu, or press **Shift+F12**.

3 If this is the first time you've saved the worksheet, type its file name and press Enter.

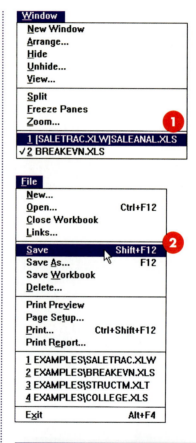

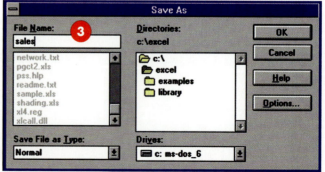

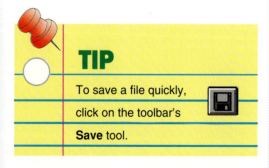

TIP

To save a file quickly, click on the toolbar's **Save** tool.

32

SAVING A WORKSHEET WITH A DIFFERENT NAME

Why Specify a Different Name?

You often need to save a worksheet under a new name. You might want to do this so you can have two copies of the same sheet (one for experimentation) or because you started a new sheet and need to give it a name other than the default name Excel assigned to it (that is, Sheet1). To save a worksheet under a new name, select Save **As** from the **F**ile menu.

TIP

When you type the file name, you don't need to add the extension (which is .XLS for a worksheet). Excel adds the appropriate extension automatically.

QUICK REFRESHER

To change drives in the Save As dialog box, click on the drive, or press **Alt+V**, and then select a new drive from the list. To change directories, double-click on the directory, or press **Alt+D**, and select a new directory with the arrow keys.

LEARNING THE LINGO

File extension: Most file names end with a period followed by one to three characters. These characters, called the file name's extension, identify the file's type. For example, all Excel worksheets have the .XLS extension, whereas Excel charts have an .XLC extension and templates have an .XLT extension.

SAVING A WORKSHEET WITH A DIFFERENT NAME

Saving a Worksheet Under a New Name

1 If you have more than one worksheet open, choose the worksheet you want to save from the **Window** menu, or click anywhere within the window.

2 Select Save **As** from the File menu, or press **F12**.

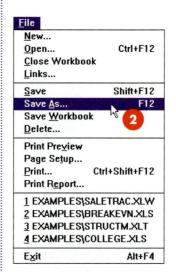

3 (Optional) Change the drive and/or directory if you want.

4 Type the new file name, and press **Enter**.

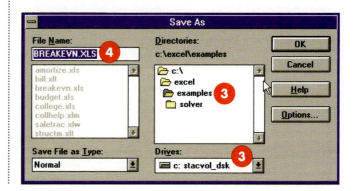

34

DELETING A WORKSHEET

Why Delete a Worksheet?

As you work with Excel, you will accumulate many worksheet files, some of which may be obsolete. Not only do these obsolete files clutter up your disk drive, but they also make it difficult to find the files you want. When you're sure you no longer need a worksheet, you can delete it from your disk drive by selecting **Delete** from the **File** menu.

Deleting a Worksheet

1 Select **D**elete from the **F**ile menu.

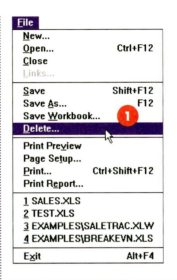

2 If needed, change the drive and/or directory to the one that contains the file to delete.

3 Double-click on the file you want to delete.

4 Select **Y**es, or press **Enter**.

5 Select **C**lose.

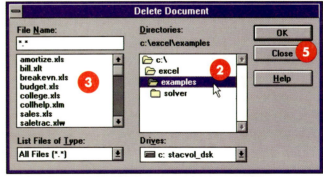

QUICK REFRESHER

To change drives in the Delete Document dialog box, click on the drive or press **Alt+V**, then select a new drive from the list. To change directories, double-click on the directory or press **Alt+D** and select a new directory with the arrow keys.

Beginning Excel Tasks

QUITTING EXCEL

Why Quit Excel?

When you're finished working with Excel, you'll want to quit the application, which closes Excel's main window and removes the program from your computer's memory. You should always end your Excel sessions this way. Never end your session by turning off your computer, as you could lose unsaved work and possibly even damage data on your hard disk.

Quitting Excel

1. Select **Exit** from the **File** menu, or press **Alt+F4**.

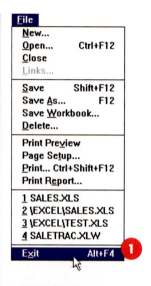

2. If prompted, select **Yes** to save the changes or **No** to quit Excel without saving the changes.

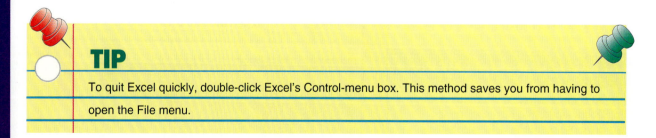

TIP

To quit Excel quickly, double-click Excel's Control-menu box. This method saves you from having to open the File menu.

PART 2

Building a Worksheet

This part describes Excel tasks that you need to know to build and manipulate worksheets. When you have finished this part, you will be able to enter data of various types into the worksheet, create mathematical functions, and edit cells.

- Selecting Cells
- Entering Labels
- Entering Values
- Entering Dates and Times
- Entering Formulas
- Using Cell References in Formulas
- Using Cell Ranges in Formulas
- Using Excel's Built-In Functions

SELECTING CELLS

Why Select Cells?

Most operations that you can perform on a single cell you can also perform on groups of cells. Simply select the group of cells before issuing the command. You can select rows, columns, rectangular blocks, or entire worksheets.

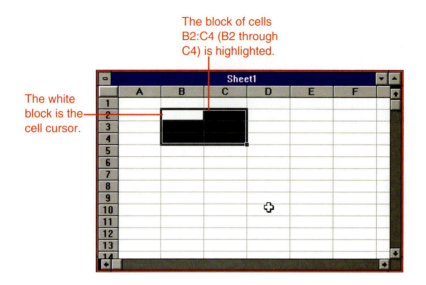

The block of cells B2:C4 (B2 through C4) is highlighted.

The white block is the cell cursor.

Selecting Groups of Cells

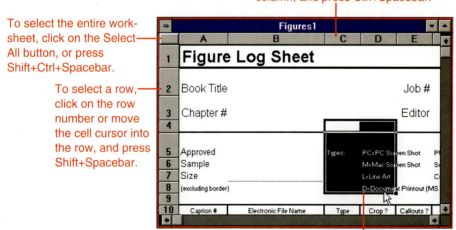

To select a column, click on the column letter, or move the cell cursor into the column, and press Ctrl+Spacebar.

To select the entire worksheet, click on the Select All button, or press Shift+Ctrl+Spacebar.

To select a row, click on the row number or move the cell cursor into the row, and press Shift+Spacebar.

To select a block of cells, drag the mouse pointer across the cells. Or move the cell cursor to the first cell, hold down Shift, and use the arrow keys to expand the block.

SELECTING CELLS

Exercise

Practice the cell-selection techniques by selecting a block of cells ranging from B2 to F10.

1 Click on cell **B2**, or use the arrow keys to position the cell cursor there.

2 Hold down the left mouse button, and move the mouse pointer to cell F10, then release the mouse button. Or hold down **Shift** and use the arrow keys to position the cell cursor at **F10**.

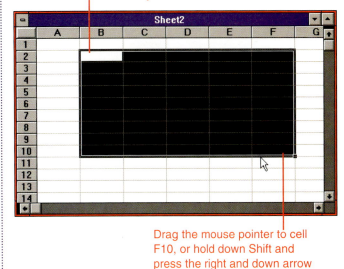

Start the block here by clicking or positioning the cell cursor with the arrow keys.

Drag the mouse pointer to cell F10, or hold down Shift and press the right and down arrow keys until F10 is highlighted.

QUICK REFRESHER

To *drag* the mouse pointer, hold down the left mouse button while you move the mouse, dragging the pointer across the screen.

39

ENTERING LABELS

What Is a Label?

The cells that make up a worksheet can hold several types of data, including labels, values, and formulas. Labels are entries that cannot be calculated, such as text in row and column headings and explanatory notes. You'll learn about values and formulas later in this book.

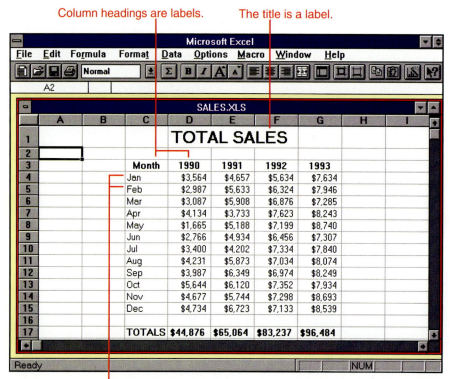

Column headings are labels.
The title is a label.
Row headings are labels.

TIP

You cannot always rely on the rule that letters are labels and numbers are values; for example, a phone number is text.

TIP

The *formula bar* always displays the contents of the current cell. In the case of text, the cell and the formula bar show the same thing. However, when the current cell contains a formula, the formula bar displays the formula, and the cell displays the value calculated by the formula. You'll learn more about formulas later in the book.

ENTERING LABELS

Entering a Label into a Cell

1 Move the cell cursor to the cell.

2 Type the label, and then press **Enter**.

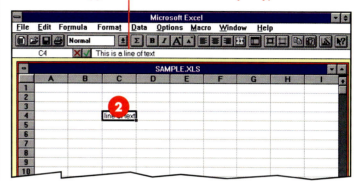

Text appears in the formula bar as you type.

LEARNING THE LINGO

Label: A series of characters that have no numerical value. A label is usually used for headings and notations.

TIP

When you enter a number into a cell, Excel assumes the number is a value rather than a label. This assumption creates problems when you need to enter a number like a zip code, which should be treated as text. Luckily, there's an easy way to tell Excel when a number is a text value. Simply begin the text entry with a single quote ('), which is the symbol to the left of your Enter key.

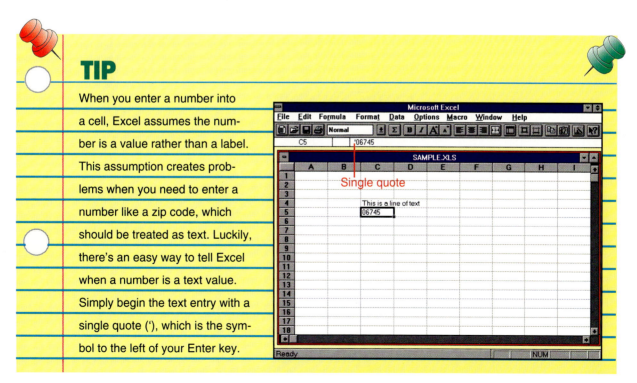

Single quote

ENTERING VALUES

What Is a Value?

A *value*, simply stated, is a number upon which you can perform a calculation. (Numbers such as ZIP codes and phone numbers are considered labels rather than values because they're not used in calculations.)

Manipulating values is the whole reason for setting up a worksheet in the first place. No matter what type of worksheet you create, sooner or later you're going to need to enter values into cells. Other cells in your worksheet then use these values in formulas to calculate the results you need. You'll learn how to enter formulas later in the book.

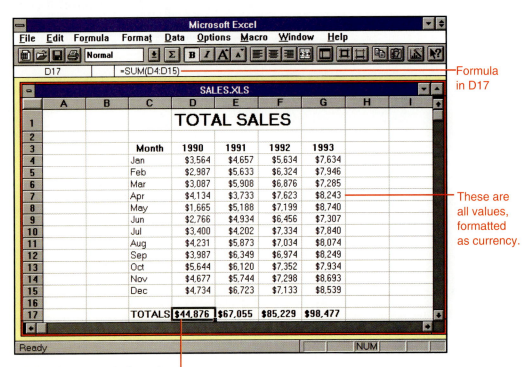

Formula in D17

These are all values, formatted as currency.

This value is the result of a formula, as you can see by looking at the formula bar.

QUICK REFRESHER

If you want Excel to interpret a number as text rather than a value, you must precede the number with a single quote (').

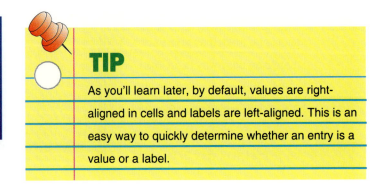

TIP

As you'll learn later, by default, values are right-aligned in cells and labels are left-aligned. This is an easy way to quickly determine whether an entry is a value or a label.

ENTERING VALUES

Entering a Value into a Cell

1 Move the cell cursor to the cell.

2 Type the value, and press **Enter**.

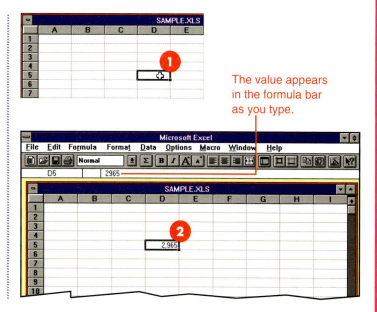

The value appears in the formula bar as you type.

Exercise

To see the difference between a regular number and a text number, type the number **08764** with and without a single quote.

1 Move to the cell.

2 Type **08764**, and press **Enter**.

3 Move to a different cell.

4 Type **'08764** (starting with a single quote), and press **Enter**.

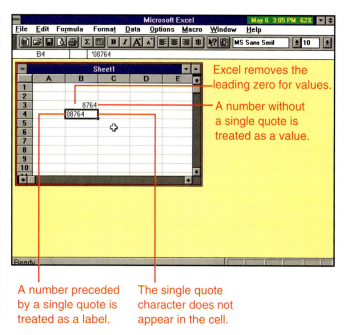

Excel removes the leading zero for values.

A number without a single quote is treated as a value.

A number preceded by a single quote is treated as a label.

The single quote character does not appear in the cell.

43

ENTERING DATES AND TIMES

How Does Excel Handle Dates and Times?

Excel treats dates and times as values, so that you can perform calculations on them. To make the dates more readable than plain values, however, Excel offers some special formatting features. When you enter a date or time, Excel attempts to match it with one of its standard formats, adding capital letters and punctuation where necessary.

You can enter and display dates in any of these formats.

Date Formats	Time Formats
5/14/93	1:30 PM
14-May-93	1:30:00 PM
14-May	13:30
May-93	13:30:00

You can show times in any of these formats.

TIP
You don't have to type a date or time exactly in the format expected by Excel. Excel will determine the format that most closely matches what you've typed and change your entry accordingly. For example, if you enter **may 14**, Excel automatically displays the date as **14-May**.

TIP
Excel stores each date and time in a plain numerical format representing its relationship to January 1, 1900. For example, January 1, 1901, 5:30 PM, would be 367.729. However, Excel realizes that you would rather see dates and times in a more readable format, so it formats them for screen display as you are accustomed to seeing them.

ENTERING DATES AND TIMES

Entering a Date or Time

1 Move to the cell.

2 Type the date or time, and press **Enter**.

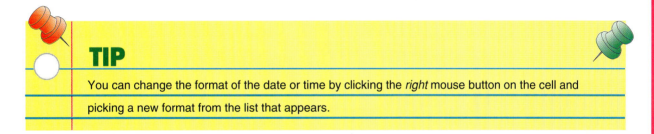

The date or time appears in the formula bar as you type.

TIP

You can change the format of the date or time by clicking the *right* mouse button on the cell and picking a new format from the list that appears.

ENTERING FORMULAS

What Is a Formula?

A *formula* is an instruction to perform some math calculation on the values in one or more cells. The formulas you enter into your worksheet may be as simple as the sum of two cells or as complex as determining the standard deviation of a table of values.

Formulas can include various elements, including values, cell references, operators, or worksheet functions. These elements are calculated based on rules of *operator precedence*, which dictate in what order various math operations are performed. You can change the order of operations by adding parentheses to a formula so that whatever is within the parentheses is calculated first.

Order	Symbol	Meaning
1	^	exponentiation
2	*/	multiplication and division
3	+-	addition and subtraction

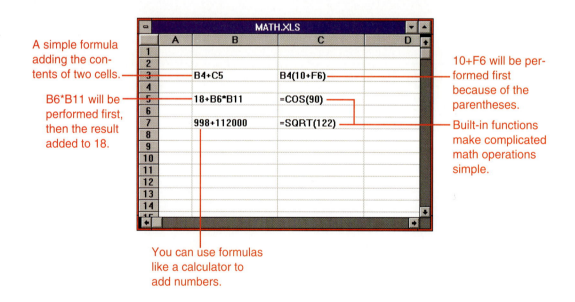

A simple formula adding the contents of two cells.

B6*B11 will be performed first, then the result added to 18.

You can use formulas like a calculator to add numbers.

10+F6 will be performed first because of the parentheses.

Built-in functions make complicated math operations simple.

ENTERING FORMULAS

Entering a Formula

1 Move to the cell.

2 Type an equals sign (=), and then the formula.

The formula appears in the formula bar as you type.

All formulas begin with an equals sign.

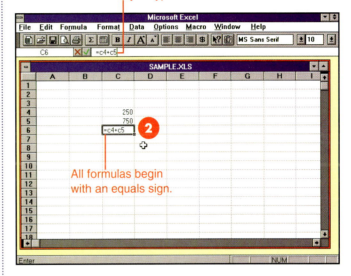

3 Press **Enter** to display the formula result in the cell.

The formula still appears in the formula bar.

The formula result appears in the cell.

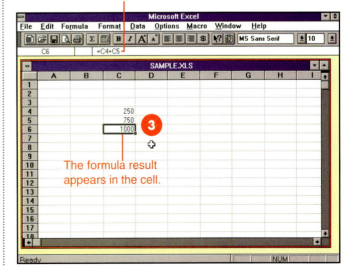

ENTERING FORMULAS

Exercise

In this exercise, you'll average the values in three cells using Excel's math operators.

1 Enter **234** in cell D3.

2 Enter **365** in cell D4.

3 Enter **419** in cell D5.

4 Enter **Average:** in cell C7.

5 Move to cell D7.

6 Type the formula **=(D3+D4+D5)/3** and press **Enter**.

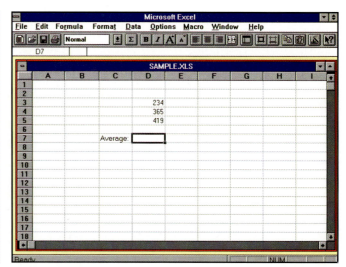

LEARNING THE LINGO

Cell reference: You create a cell reference by typing the cell's column letter followed by the cell's row number (that is, **B12**).

Operators: Excel supports many operators that you can use in your formulas, including addition (+), subtraction (-), multiplication (*), division (/), and percentage (%).

Worksheet functions: These are built-in functions that you can use to calculate values. Some functions are SUM, which calculates sums; AVERAGE, which calculates averages; and SQRT, which calculates square roots. There are hundreds of worksheet functions, all of which are listed in the *Function Reference* that came with your copy of Excel.

Operator precedence: The order in which arithmetic operations are performed, also called "order of operations."

TIP

The formula in the above exercise can be simplified by using Excel's SUM function. The formula would then look like **=SUM(D3:D5)/3**. To learn more about Excel's worksheet functions, refer to the "Using Excel's Built-in Functions" task later in the part.

48

USING CELL REFERENCES IN FORMULAS

Why Use Cell References in Formulas?

It's virtually impossible to create useful formulas without using cell references. For example, suppose you want to sum a column of values. You could copy the values directly into your formula, but if you later change a value, your formula will be wrong. By using cell references to tell Excel where values are stored, Excel can automatically calculate new results whenever values change.

Formula entered in A4.

QUICK REFRESHER

As you've already learned, a cell reference is comprised of a column letter and a row number. The cell at the intersection of the row and column is the cell to which you're referring.

Building a Worksheet

USING CELL REFERENCES IN FORMULAS

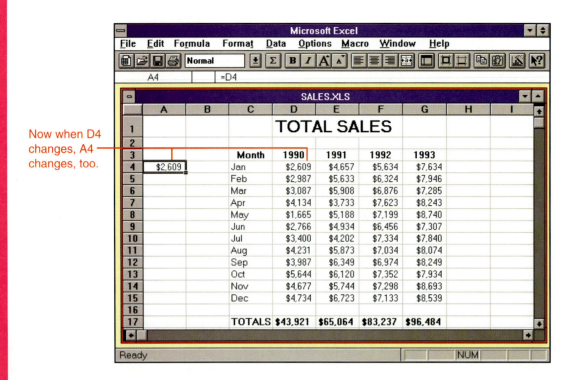

Now when D4 changes, A4 changes, too.

LEARNING THE LINGO

Cell reference: A column letter followed by a row number that refers to the value in a particular cell.

USING CELL RANGES IN FORMULAS

Why Use Ranges?

Often, you need to refer to all the cells in a block. Using two simple cell references separated by a colon (called a *cell range*), you can refer to any block of cells you like, even an entire worksheet.

Specifying Ranges

1 Type the cell reference for the upper left corner of the block.

2 Type a colon (:).

3 Type the cell reference for the lower right corner of the block.

The formula entered into D17 sums all cells from D4 down to D15.

The formula in A7 sums the values in the entire table.

LEARNING THE LINGO

Cell range: A cell range refers to a block of cells and consists of two cell references separated by a colon.

Building a Worksheet

51

USING EXCEL'S BUILT-IN FUNCTIONS

What Are Functions?

If you look in the *Function Reference* that came with your copy of Excel, you'll see that Excel provides hundreds of functions you can use to simplify calculations in your worksheets. For example, while you can sum a series of cells by typing a formula like **=A1+A2+A3+A4+A5**, it's much easier to use Excel's SUM function: **SUM(A1:A5)**.

Functions are made up of a function name followed by the function's arguments enclosed in parentheses. Multiple arguments are separated by commas. Function arguments can be just about any type of data, depending on the function. You'll mostly use numbers, cell references, formulas, and possibly text as arguments.

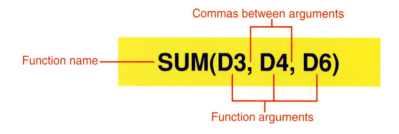

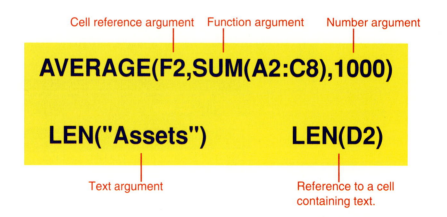

QUICK REFRESHER

Remember, if a function appears at the beginning of a formula, it must start with an equals (=) sign.

LEARNING THE LINGO

Arguments: The values functions need in order to calculate a result. A function's arguments are enclosed in parentheses.

USING EXCEL'S BUILT-IN FUNCTIONS

Pasting a Function into a Worksheet

1 Move to the cell into which you want to paste the function.

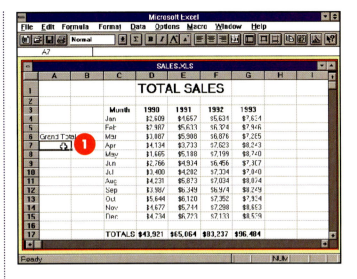

2 Select Paste Function from the Formula menu.

3 Select a category from the Function Category list box.

4 Select a function from the Paste Function list box.

5 Choose **OK**.

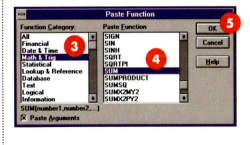

6 Finish the formula by typing the arguments needed.

Building a Worksheet

USING EXCEL'S BUILT-IN FUNCTIONS

Exercise

Practice using functions by pasting into A5 a function that calculates the average of cells B5, C8, and D5 through E10.

1 Move to cell **A5**.

2 Select Pa**s**te Function from the Fo**r**mula menu.

3 Choose **Statistical** from the Function **C**ategory list box.

4 Choose **AVERAGE** from the Paste **F**unction list box.

5 Choose **OK**.

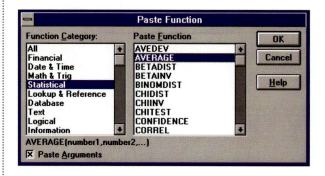

6 Type the arguments **B8,C8,D5:E10**.

7 Press **Del** until the characters **,number2,...** are deleted from the function bar. (Make sure you don't delete the right hand parenthesis.)

8 Press **Enter**.

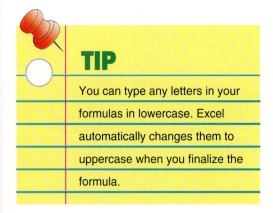

TIP

You can type any letters in your formulas in lowercase. Excel automatically changes them to uppercase when you finalize the formula.

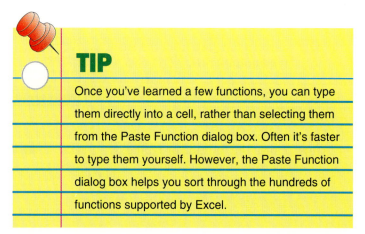

TIP

Once you've learned a few functions, you can type them directly into a cell, rather than selecting them from the Paste Function dialog box. Often it's faster to type them yourself. However, the Paste Function dialog box helps you sort through the hundreds of functions supported by Excel.

PART 3
Editing and Formatting a Worksheet

This part describes how to change your worksheet's contents and format. When you have finished this part, you will be able to copy, move, insert, delete, find, and sort cells; change cell formats; adjust the alignment of cell data; and modify cell widths and heights.

- Editing Cell Contents
- Moving and Copying Cells
- Inserting Rows and Columns
- Deleting Rows and Columns
- Clearing Cells
- Finding Data in Cells
- Replacing Data in Cells
- Sorting Data
- Changing Number Formats
- Aligning Data in Cells
- Changing Cell Widths
- Changing Fonts and Text Attributes

EDITING CELL CONTENTS

Why Edit Cell Contents?

Worksheets can grow to contain dozens, even hundreds, of values and formulas. Sooner or later, you'll discover an error in a cell or need to update a formula to reflect changes in the worksheet. Luckily, editing the contents of a cell is as easy as editing a document with a word processor. You only need to select the cell to edit and then change the contents of the cell in the formula bar.

Editing Cell Contents

1 Move to the cell whose contents you want to edit.

The contents of the selected cell appear in the formula bar.

EDITING CELL CONTENTS

2 Click on the formula bar, or press **F2**.

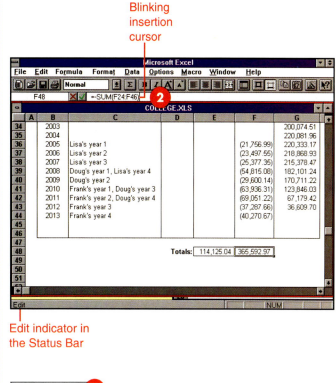

Blinking insertion cursor

Edit indicator in the Status Bar

3 Edit the entry, and press **Enter** when you're finished.

LEARNING THE LINGO

Insertion cursor: A blinking vertical bar that shows where the next typed character will appear.

Status Bar: An area at the bottom of Excel's main window that displays messages about the worksheet's status.

57

MOVING AND COPYING CELLS

Why Move or Copy Cells?

As you manipulate a worksheet, you may need to copy or move blocks of data to different locations. For example, you might want to do this to reorganize the way a worksheet is laid out, or you might want to start a table that contains similar data to an existing table.

When you move or copy formulas that contain cell references, you don't have to worry about changing the cell references in your formula; the formula changes to take its new location into account. For example, if you have **=B2+B3** in cell B4, and move the formula to cell D4, the formula becomes **=D2+D3**.

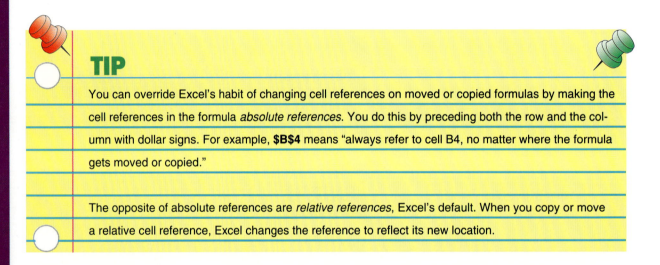

TIP

You can override Excel's habit of changing cell references on moved or copied formulas by making the cell references in the formula *absolute references*. You do this by preceding both the row and the column with dollar signs. For example, **$B$4** means "always refer to cell B4, no matter where the formula gets moved or copied."

The opposite of absolute references are *relative references*, Excel's default. When you copy or move a relative cell reference, Excel changes the reference to reflect its new location.

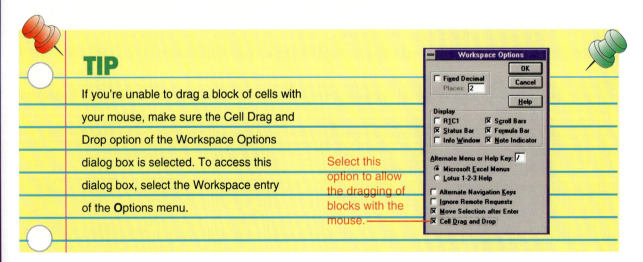

TIP

If you're unable to drag a block of cells with your mouse, make sure the Cell Drag and Drop option of the Workspace Options dialog box is selected. To access this dialog box, select the Workspace entry of the **O**ptions menu.

Select this option to allow the dragging of blocks with the mouse.

58

MOVING AND COPYING CELLS

Moving or Copying Cells

1. Move to the upper left cell in the block you want to move.

2. Holding down the left mouse button, drag the mouse pointer to the lower right cell of the block.

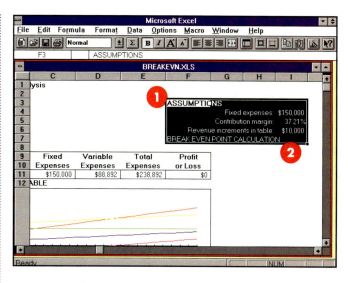

3. (Optional) If you are copying (rather than moving), hold down **Ctrl** while you perform the next step.

4. Move the mouse cursor to the edge of the highlighted block, and hold down the left mouse button while you drag the block to its new location.

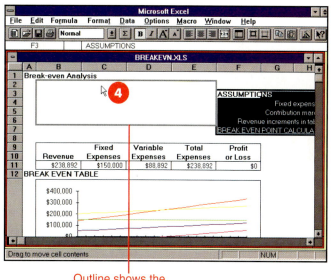

Outline shows the destination.

Editing and Formatting a Worksheet

59

MOVING AND COPYING CELLS

Exercise

Create the simple worksheet shown in this figure. Then move the block of data from **B3:D5** to **C20:E22**.

Using the mouse:

1 Move to cell **B3**.

2 Holding down the left mouse button, drag the mouse pointer to **D5**, and then release the mouse button.

3 Move the mouse pointer to one of the block's edges.

4 Hold down the left mouse button and drag the block to position its upper left corner at **C20**. Then release the mouse button.

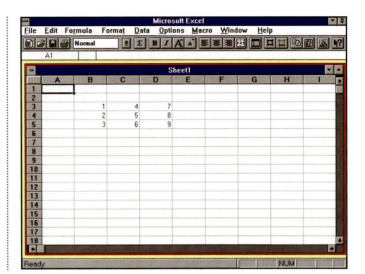

TIP

You can also move and copy with the keyboard. Highlight the block by holding down **Shift** while you extend the highlight across the cells. Press **Ctrl+X** to cut the block or **Ctrl+C** to copy it, move to the upper left corner of the new location, and press **Enter**.

INSERTING ROWS AND COLUMNS

Why Insert Rows and Columns?

The more complicated a worksheet becomes, the more likely it is that you will need to make changes—adding new data. You can easily add entire rows or columns of cells by using Excel's Insert command. When you add cells, Excel automatically adjusts moved cell references to reflect their new location.

Before you insert a row or column, you must indicate where you want it. Do this by selecting an existing row or column that's to the right or below the location where you want the new one. Use this table as a guideline:

To select	Use the mouse	Or the keyboard
A row	Click on the row number	Press **Shift+Spacebar** while cell cursor is in the row.
A column	Click the column letter	Press **Ctrl+Spacebar** while cell cursor is in the column.

INSERTING ROWS AND COLUMNS

Inserting a Row or Column

1 Select the row or column below or to the right of where you want the new row or column (see the table on page 61).

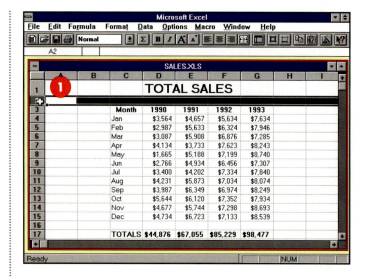

2 Select **Insert** from the **Edit** menu.

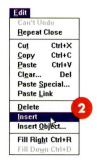

62

DELETING ROWS AND COLUMNS

Why Delete Rows and Columns?

If you find that a column you've created in your worksheet is not needed, you can simply delete it. All remaining columns shift, and cell references are automatically adjusted.

You must select the row or column to delete before you can remove it. Use this table as a guideline:

To select	Use the mouse	Or the keyboard
A row	Click on the row number	Press **Shift+Spacebar** while cell cursor is in the row.
A column	Click the column letter	Press **Ctrl+Spacebar** while cell cursor is in the column.

TIP

Although you can add or delete individual cells, this is a risky operation, since you may inadvertently disorganize tables of data. It's a good rule to insert only entire rows and columns.

DELETING ROWS AND COLUMNS

Deleting a Row or Column

1 Select the row or column you want to delete (see the table on page 63).

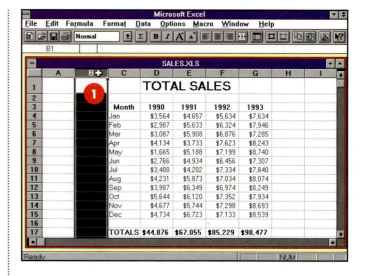

2 Select **D**elete from the **E**dit menu.

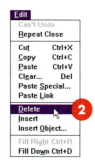

CLEARING CELLS

Why Clear Cells?

Once you enter data into a cell, you're not stuck with it forever. Excel allows you to clear data, formats, or notes from any cell at any time.

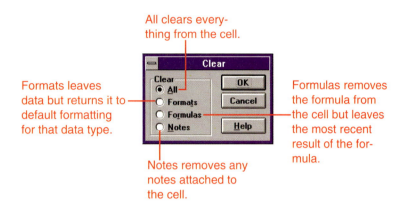

All clears everything from the cell.

Formats leaves data but returns it to default formatting for that data type.

Formulas removes the formula from the cell but leaves the most recent result of the formula.

Notes removes any notes attached to the cell.

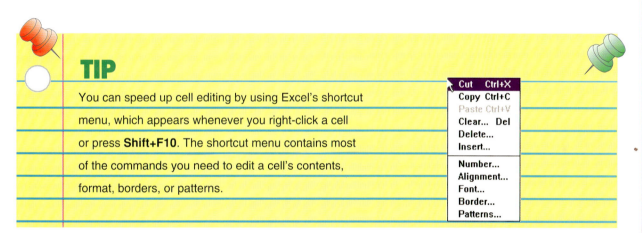

TIP

You can speed up cell editing by using Excel's shortcut menu, which appears whenever you right-click a cell or press **Shift+F10**. The shortcut menu contains most of the commands you need to edit a cell's contents, format, borders, or patterns.

LEARNING THE LINGO

Cell format: A cell's format is the way a cell displays its data, including the number type, the alignment of data within the cell, and text styles, such as bold or italics.

CLEARING CELLS

Clearing a Cell

1 Move to the cell you want to clear.

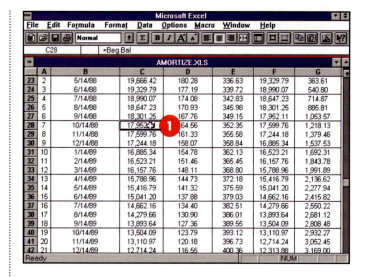

2 Select **Cl**ear from the **E**dit menu, or press **Delete**.

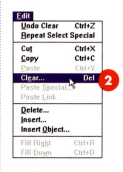

3 Select what you want cleared from the cell.

4 Select **OK**, or press **Enter**.

TIP

There's a difference between clearing and deleting. When you delete a cell, you remove both the cell and its contents from your worksheet. When you clear a cell, only the cell's contents are deleted. The cell itself remains in place. Don't let it fool you that you press the **Delete** key to clear—not delete—a cell.

66

FINDING DATA IN CELLS

Why Find Data in Cells?

While it's easy enough to edit a cell's contents on the formula bar, you may at times find that you can't locate the cell you want. For example, you may be looking for the cell that contains the grand total of the payroll account. Luckily, Excel provides an easy way to find cells.

Finding Cells Containing Specific Data

1 Select **F**ind from the Fo**r**mula menu, or press **Shift+F5**.

2 Type the data you want to find.

3 Select **OK**, or press **Enter**.

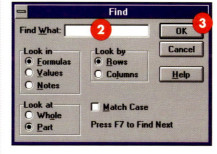

4 To find the next occurrence of the data, press **F7**.

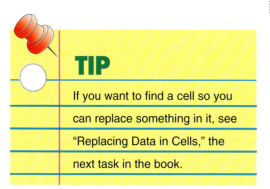

TIP

If you want to find a cell so you can replace something in it, see "Replacing Data in Cells," the next task in the book.

TIP

To limit your search to a specific block of cells, highlight the cells before you select the **F**ind command. Excel then searches only the cells in the block.

67

REPLACING DATA IN CELLS

Why Replace Data?

Replacing is handy when there are many cells you want to edit simultaneously. For example, you might want to change all occurrences of the word **Profit** to **Net Profit**. Excel provides powerful search and replace commands that make this type of editing a snap to perform.

Finding and Replacing Data

1 Select Replace from the Formula menu.

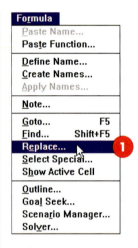

2 Type the data you want to find, press **Tab**, and type the replacement data.

3 To replace all occurrences of the data, select the Replace **All** button. Or to replace only the text in the current cell, select the **R**eplace button.

4 If you chose the **R**eplace button, continue selecting it until all the cells containing the text you want to change have been changed.

5 Select the **Close** button. (You don't need to do this if you selected Replace **All**.)

68

SORTING DATA

Why Sort Data?

Many of your worksheets will contain long lists of data. Often, you'll want to view the data in these lists in a different order. To help you do this, Excel provides a sorting function that can arrange data into alphabetical or numerical order. All you need to do is highlight the data to be sorted and select Excel's Sort command.

Sorting Rows of Data

1 Move to the upper left cell of the block of data to sort.

2 Holding down the left mouse button, drag the mouse pointer to the lower right corner of the block you want to sort.

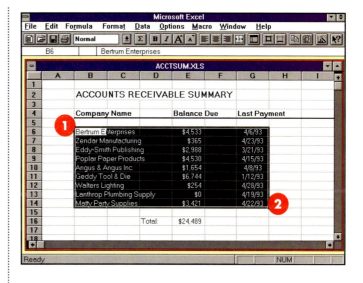

3 Select **S**ort from the **D**ata menu.

Editing and Formatting a Worksheet

SORTING DATA

4 Click on any cell in the column by which you want to sort.

5 Select **OK**, press **Enter**.

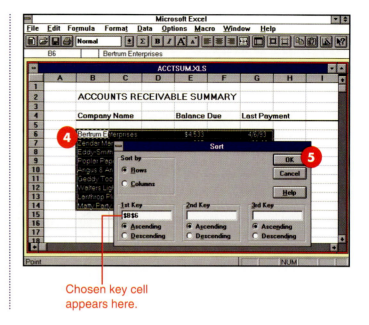

Chosen key cell appears here.

TIP

When you select a block of data to sort, make sure you include all of the related data. For example, suppose you have a worksheet containing company names and addresses. If you select only the names, when you sort the rows, the names will no longer appear next to their correct addresses.

SORTING DATA

Exercise

Create the worksheet shown in the figure, and then sort the data in order of company name. Next, sort the data in order of number of employees.

1 Move to cell **B5**.

2 Holding down the left button, drag the mouse pointer to cell **E8**.

3 Select **S**ort from the **D**ata menu.

4 Click on cell **B5**.

5 Select **OK**, or press **Enter**. Excel sorts the data according to column B.

6 Leaving the block of data highlighted, again select **S**ort from the **D**ata menu.

7 Click on cell **E5**.

8 Select **OK**, or press **Enter**. Excel sorts the data again, this time according to column E.

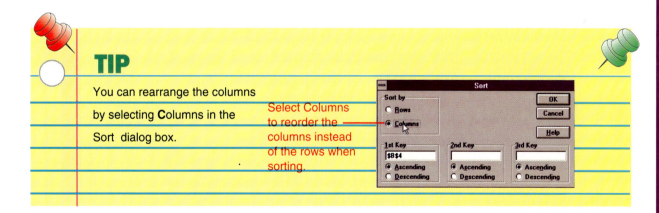

TIP

You can rearrange the columns by selecting **C**olumns in the Sort dialog box.

Select Columns to reorder the columns instead of the rows when sorting.

CHANGING NUMBER FORMATS

Why Change Number Formats?

When you type a number into a cell, Excel displays the number in the general format. But what if you want to display the value as currency? Or suppose you want a number with commas and decimal points? To format a number, you must set the cell's format type. You can do this just by typing your number in the format desired. For example, if you type $23.95, Excel knows that you want the cell formatted as currency. If you need to change the format of a cell, though, select **N**umber from the Forma**t** menu.

Changing Number Formats

1 Move to the cell for which you want to change the number format.

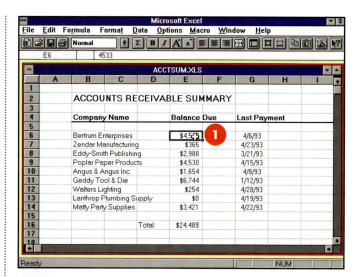

2 Select **N**umber from the Forma**t** menu.

3 Select the format category you want from the **C**ategory list.

4 Select the format you want from the **F**ormat Codes list.

5 Select **OK**, or press **Enter**.

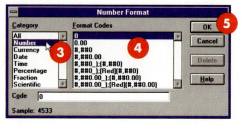

72

ALIGNING DATA IN CELLS

Why Align Data?

Besides adding format codes to your worksheet's cells, you can also add alignment information, which determines where data is displayed within a cell. You can dramatically improve the look of your worksheet with some simple alignment adjustments. Here are some examples:

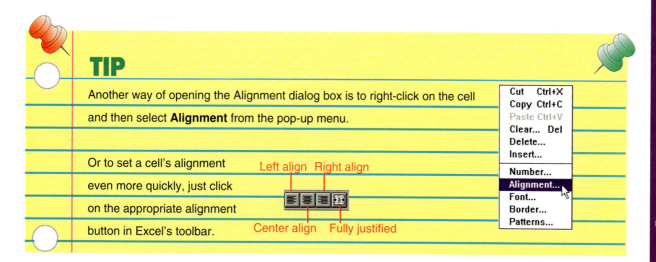

TIP

Another way of opening the Alignment dialog box is to right-click on the cell and then select **Alignment** from the pop-up menu.

Or to set a cell's alignment even more quickly, just click on the appropriate alignment button in Excel's toolbar.

LEARNING THE LINGO

Alignment: Alignment is the way data is positioned within a cell.

Orientation: Orientation is the direction in which the characters of the text are displayed.

ALIGNING DATA IN CELLS

Aligning Data

1 Move to the cell for which you want to set alignment.

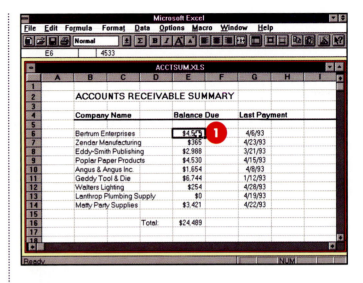

2 Select **A**lignment from the Forma**t** menu.

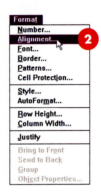

3 Select the horizontal alignment you want.

4 (Optional) Select the vertical alignment you want.

5 Select **OK**, or press **Enter**.

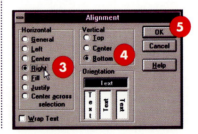

TIP

You can make text appear vertically or sideways by selecting one of the options in the Alignment dialog box's Orientation box. You might want vertical or sideways text, for example, to label the left side of a table.

74

CHANGING CELL WIDTHS

Why Adjust Cell Width?

When you type data that's too wide for a cell, Excel displays the data in one of two ways. If the data is text, and the neighboring cell is empty, Excel lets the text overrun the borders of the cell. However, if the neighboring cell is not empty, Excel cannot allow it to be covered. In this case, Excel displays only the text that fits. If the long data is a number, Excel displays a series of pound signs (########), which tells you that the value is too large. In either case, you'll want to widen the cell so that all its data can be displayed.

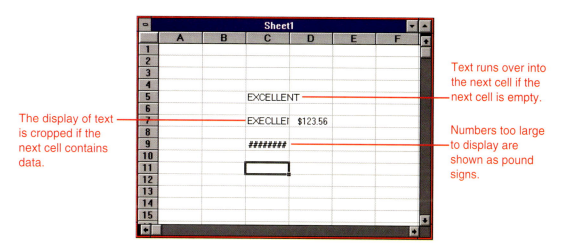

The display of text is cropped if the next cell contains data.

Text runs over into the next cell if the next cell is empty.

Numbers too large to display are shown as pound signs.

TIP

Mouse users can quickly select the best fit by double-clicking the right edge of the column heading (the 1 button containing the column letter). Or you can drag the right edge of the column heading to adjust the width manually.

Double-click on the right edge of the column's letter button to automatically adjust the width.

When you move the mouse pointer between column letter buttons, its shape changes.

Drag the column border to adjust width manually.

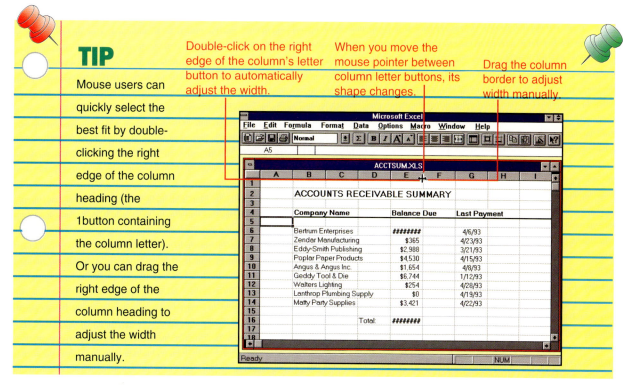

75

CHANGING CELL WIDTHS

Changing a Column's Width

1 Move to any cell in the column to change.

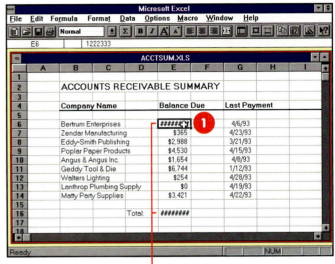

These numbers are too large to fit in their cells.

2 Select **C**olumn Width from the Forma**t** menu.

3 Type the number of characters you want to fit into the cell.

4 Select **OK**, or press **Enter**.

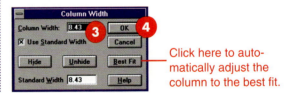

Click here to automatically adjust the column to the best fit.

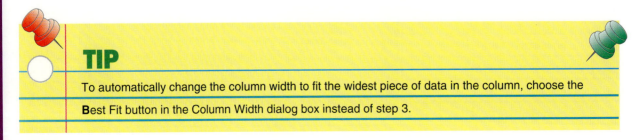

TIP

To automatically change the column width to fit the widest piece of data in the column, choose the **B**est Fit button in the Column Width dialog box instead of step 3.

76

CHANGING FONTS AND TEXT ATTRIBUTES

Why Use Different Fonts and Attributes?

While Excel's default fonts and text attributes are usually acceptable for most cells in a worksheet, you may want to call attention to cells containing titles, labels, and other significant data by displaying them with different lettering. Excel can display text using any Windows font. In addition, you can assign one or more of three text attributes (bold, italic, and underlined) to text. All of these features are available from Excel's Format menu.

LEARNING THE LINGO

Font: A set of characters, all of which belong to the same design family.

Text Styles: Attributes such as bold, italic, and underlining that can be applied to text.

TIP

You can select the bold and italic text styles, as well as increase or decrease the font size, by clicking on the appropriate buttons in Excel's toolbar.

Editing and Formatting a Worksheet

CHANGING FONTS AND TEXT ATTRIBUTES

Changing Fonts and Attributes

1 Move to the cell for which you want to change the font.

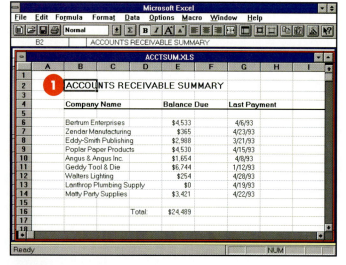

2 Select **F**ont from the Forma**t** menu.

3 Choose the font you want from the **F**ont list.

4 Choose the text attributes you want from the Font S**t**yle box.

5 Choose the lettering size you want from the **S**ize box.

6 Select **OK**, or press **Enter**.

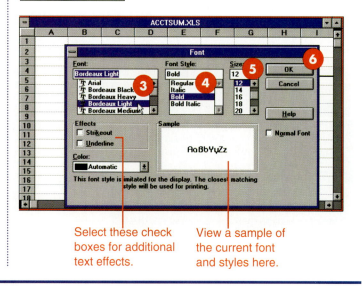

Select these check boxes for additional text effects.

View a sample of the current font and styles here.

78

PART 4

Charting Data in a Worksheet

This part describes how to display worksheet data in chart form. Because charts are often easier to understand than long lists of numbers, you can easily evaluate portions of your worksheets as a chart. When you have finished this part, you will be able to create several types of charts; delete charts; edit charts; and add labels, notes, and legends to charts.

- Creating a Chart with ChartWizard
- Changing a Chart's Type
- Giving a Chart Its Own Window
- Editing a Chart with ChartWizard
- Changing Values on a Chart
- Adding a Chart Legend
- Deleting Chart Elements
- Clearing a Data Series or Format
- Deleting an Embedded Chart

CREATING A CHART WITH CHARTWIZARD

What Is ChartWizard?

Creating a chart can be a meticulous process, but Excel provides a special tool called *ChartWizard* that does much of the chart-creating work for you. ChartWizard guides you every step of the way through the creation of your chart, making it possible to design a sophisticated chart with only a few mouse clicks. You start ChartWizard by clicking its button on Excel's toolbar.

Creating a Chart with Chart Wizard

1 Move to the upper left corner of the block you want to convert to a chart.

2 Holding down the left mouse button, drag the mouse pointer to the lower right corner of the block.

3 Click on the **ChartWizard** button in Excel's toolbar.

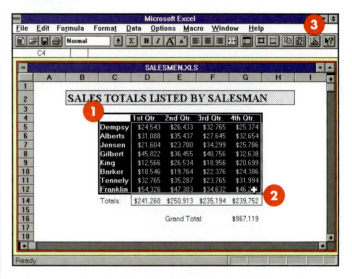

4 Click where you want the upper left corner of the chart to be, and then drag the mouse pointer in order to outline the size of the chart.

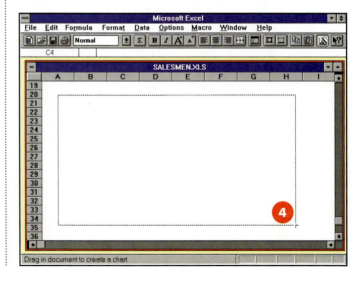

80

CREATING A CHART WITH CHARTWIZARD

5 Select **Next**.

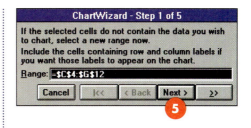

6 Click on the chart type you want, and then select **Next**.

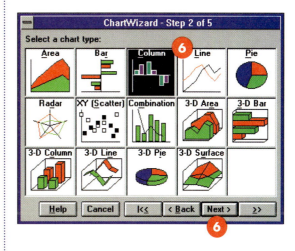

7 Click on the chart format you want, and select **Next**.

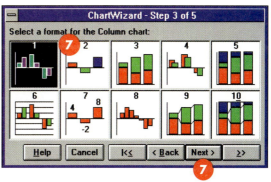

8 Select options until the sample chart appears the way you want yours to look, and then select **Next**.

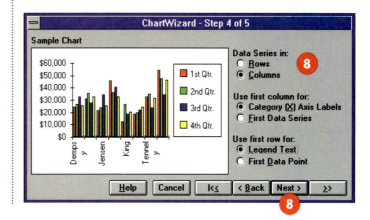

81

Charting Data in a Worksheet

CREATING A CHART WITH CHARTWIZARD

9 Select **Yes** or **No** to choose whether a legend will be used.

10 (Optional) Type a title under **Chart Titles**.

11 Select **OK**.

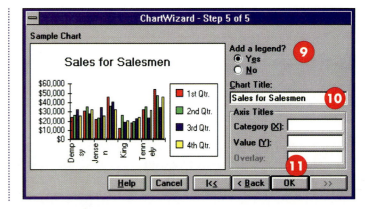

LEARNING THE LINGO

Legend: A chart legend tells you what the different parts of a chart mean.

TIP

When you highlight a block of data for a chart, include the data's labels, and ChartWizard will automatically add the labels to the chart.

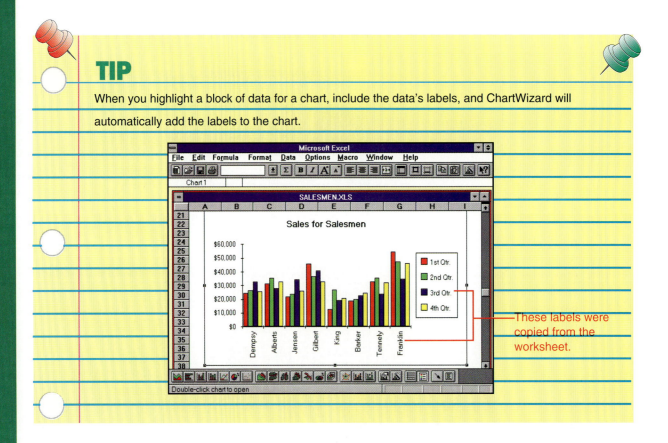

These labels were copied from the worksheet.

82

CREATING A CHART WITH CHARTWIZARD

Exercise

In this exercise, you'll create a simple worksheet and then create a bar chart from the data.

1 Enter the data shown in the figure.

2 Click on cell **B3**.

3 Holding down the left mouse button, drag the mouse pointer down to **C15**.

4 Click on the **ChartWizard** button in Excel's toolbar.

5 Click on cell **E4**, and, holding down the left mouse button, drag the mouse pointer to cell **I16**.

6 Select **Next** in the Step 1 dialog box.

7 Select **Next** in the Step 2 dialog box.

8 Select **Next** in the Step 3 dialog box.

9 Select **Next** in the Step 4 dialog box.

10 In the Step 5 dialog box, click on **No** for a chart legend, and then select **OK**.

11 Save the worksheet to use in later exercises. Use the file name **SAVED.XLS**.

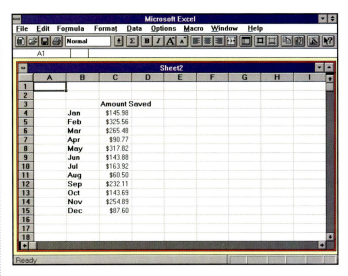

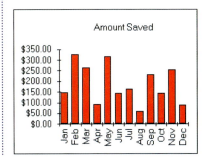

QUICK REFRESHER

To save a file, select **S**ave from the **F**ile menu.

Charting Data in a Worksheet

CHANGING A CHART'S TYPE

Why Change the Chart Type?

Once you've created your chart with ChartWizard, you can change the chart any way you like. While the chart is on the screen, you might, for example, want to experiment with different chart types, to see which type best displays the data. Changing the chart type is so easy, you should switch among many types until you find the type best suited to your needs.

Click on	To Create	Click on	To Create
	area chart		3D pie chart
	horizontal bar chart		3D surface chart
	vertical bar chart		radar chart
	stacked bar chart		combination line and bar chart
	line chart		high-low-close stock chart
	pie chart		
	scatter chart	**Click on**	**To:**
	3D area chart		Restore chart to preferred format
	3D horizontal bar chart		Create or to edit a chart
	3D vertical bar chart		Toggle chart gridlines on and off
	3D perspective bar chart		Add or delete a chart legend
	3D line chart		Draw an arrow on the chart
			Add text to a chart

CHANGING A CHART'S TYPE

Changing a Chart's Type

1 Click on the chart to select it.

2 In the chart's toolbar, click on the button for the type of chart you want.

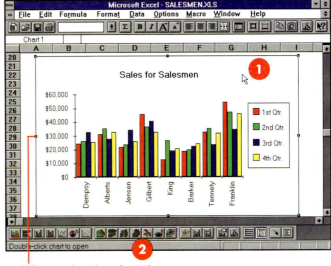

When a chart is selected, its handles appear.

TIP

Different types of charts emphasize data in different ways. For example, the pie chart in this figure differs from a bar chart in that it directly compares the total sales made by each salesman. If you wanted to show the best salespeople, the pie chart would be a better choice than the bar chart.

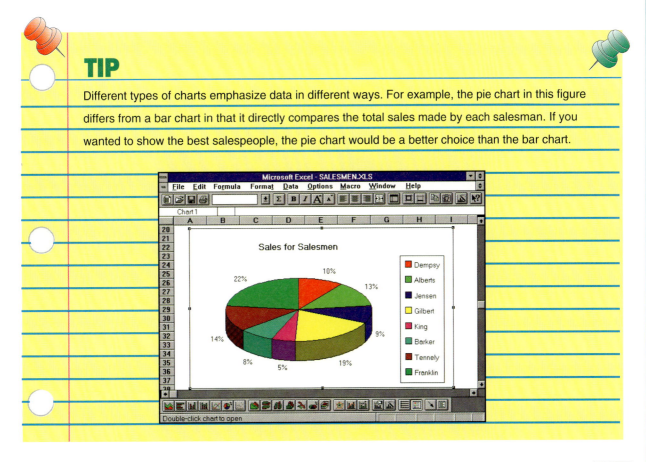

GIVING A CHART ITS OWN WINDOW

Why Give a Chart Its Own Window?

Excel's ChartWizard tool creates *embedded charts*, charts which are part of the worksheet. You cannot save these charts independently of the worksheet, and there are limitations on the editing you can perform on them. *Chart documents*, on the other hand, are charts that have their own windows and that can be saved to their own files and edited using a full range of tools and commands.

Changing an embedded chart to a chart document is easy. Just double-click on the chart, and it appears in its own window. Then, any changes you make to the chart document also appear on the embedded chart.

Changing an Embedded Chart to a Chart Document

1 Double-click on the chart.

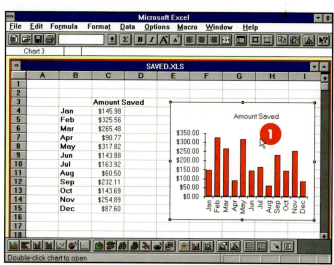

GIVING A CHART ITS OWN WINDOW

2 Select Save **As** from the **F**ile menu.

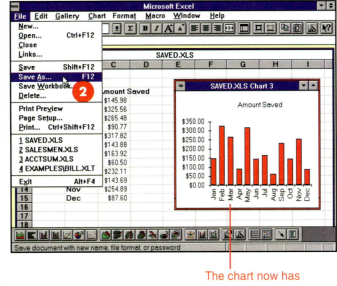

The chart now has its own window.

3 Type a name for the chart, and press **Enter**. (If you want to keep the default name, just press **Enter** without typing anything.)

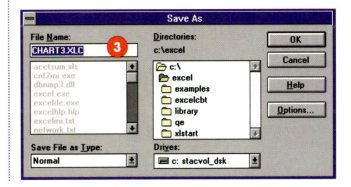

LEARNING THE LINGO

Embedded chart: An embedded chart is part of a worksheet.

Chart document: A chart document is not part of a worksheet and has its own window.

87

EDITING A CHART WITH CHARTWIZARD

When Would I Edit a Chart?

As you add data to a worksheet, you may also find that you need to add the data to your charts. Just as you used ChartWizard to create the charts, so can you use ChartWizard to edit the charts' contents. Using ChartWizard, you can add new data to the chart or change the way the data is displayed.

Editing a Chart with ChartWizard

1 Click on the chart you want to edit.

2 Click on the ChartWizard button on the Chart toolbar.

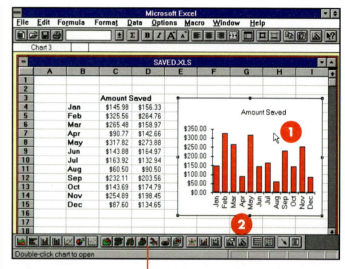

When you click on the chart, the chart toolbar appears.

3 Edit the **R**ange to include any new data you want in the chart, and then select Next.

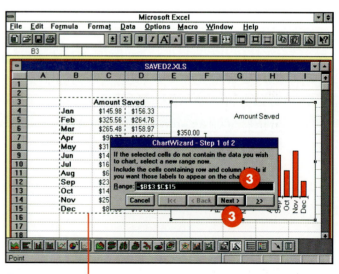

The outline shows the data that is currently displayed in the chart.

88

EDITING A CHART WITH CHARTWIZARD

4 Click on the display options to create the type of chart you want, and then select **OK**.

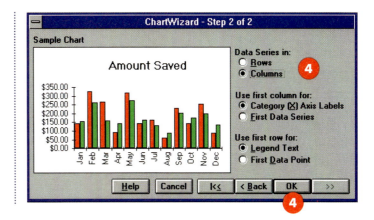

TIP

Some ChartWizard dialog boxes show how your chart looks with the currently set options. You can easily experiment with different options, by selecting the options and seeing how they change the sample chart. In this way, you may discover a better way to represent the data on your chart.

Exercise

Load the worksheet and chart named **SAVED.XLS** that you created in the first task in this part. Then add the second column of data shown in the figure here. (You can use whatever numbers you like.) Then follow the steps in this exercise to add the new data to the chart.

1 Click on the chart.

2 On the chart toolbar, click on the **ChartWizard** button.

3 In the Range text box, change the range to **$B$3:$D$15**, and then click on the **Next** button.

4 In the Step 2 dialog box, select **OK**.

5 Save the newly edited chart for use in later exercises. Name it **SAVED2.XLS**.

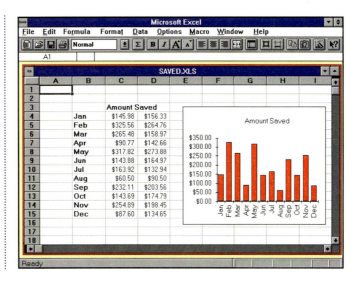

CHANGING VALUES ON A CHART

Why Change Values?

Worksheets are often used to perform projections on data to see what might happen if a certain situation occurred. One way to experiment with values in this way is to simply change the cells in the worksheet to see how the change affects other cells. However, if the data with which you want to experiment is also displayed in a chart, you can use your mouse to modify the chart, which also changes the associated values in the worksheet.

Changing Data Values on a Chart

1. If necessary, double-click the chart to create a chart document.

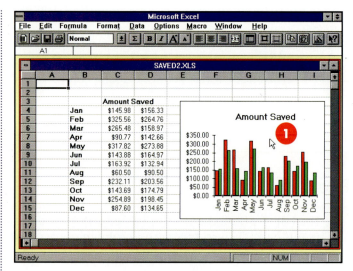

2. Hold down **Ctrl**, and click on the data marker you want to change.

CHANGING VALUES ON A CHART

3 Drag the data marker to its new position.

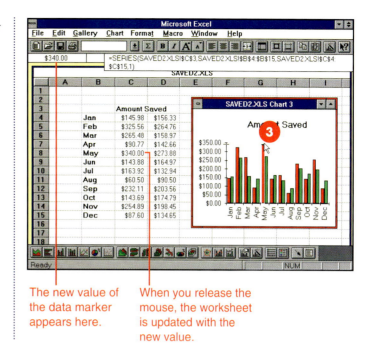

The new value of the data marker appears here.

When you release the mouse, the worksheet is updated with the new value.

LEARNING THE LINGO

Data marker: A data marker represents a value in a chart. For example, in a bar chart, the data markers are the bars, whereas in a pie chart, the data markers are the pie slices.

Charting Data in a Worksheet

ADDING A CHART LEGEND

Why Use Legends?

Legends are another element you can use to make a chart more understandable and are especially important when a chart displays multiple data series. When ChartWizard creates a chart with multiple data series, it plots each data series in its own color. The legend then shows which color goes with which data series, information that can be critical in order to correctly interpret the chart.

LEARNING THE LINGO

Data series: A data series in a chart is equivalent to a column of data in a worksheet. For example, a chart created from a two-column table will usually have two data series, each plotted with its own color.

Adding a Chart Legend

1. Type column titles on the worksheet.

2. Click on the chart to select it.

3. Click on the **Legend** tool in the Chart toolbar.

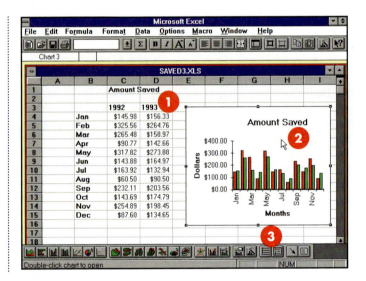

92

ADDING A CHART LEGEND

Exercise

Load the worksheet and chart named **SAVED3.XLS** that you created in the previous task. Then create the legend shown in the figure.

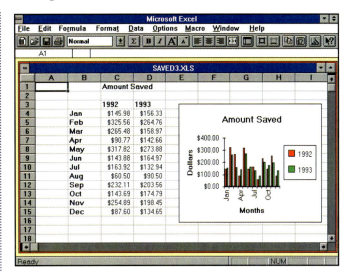

1 Delete the text **Amount Saved** from the worksheet.

2 Add the column titles **1992** and **1993** to the worksheet, as shown in the figure. (Remember to start these text labels with a single quote.)

3 Click on the chart to select it.

4 Click on the **Legend** tool on the Chart toolbar.

5 Retype the text **Amount Saved**, only now place it in cell **C1**.

6 Save the newly edited worksheet and chart for upcoming exercises. Name it **SAVED4.XLS**.

DELETING CHART ELEMENTS

Why Delete Chart Elements?

As you experiment with different chart layouts, you may want to delete elements that don't work quite right for your purposes. Deleting chart elements, such as titles and legends, is as easy as selecting an element, and pressing the keyboard's Delete key. When you delete a chart element, you completely remove it from the chart.

Deleting Chart Elements

1. If necessary, double-click the chart, creating a chart document.

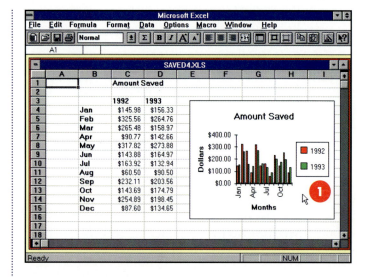

2. Click on the chart element you want to delete, and press the keyboard's **Delete** key.

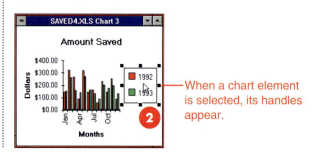

When a chart element is selected, its handles appear.

CLEARING A DATA SERIES OR FORMAT

Why Clear a Data Series or Format?

Sometimes, you need to modify a chart's data elements in order to show different data relationships. For example, in a chart that displays sales for two years, you might want to clear the older data series so that only the most recent year appears on the chart. You might also want to change the format in which the data is displayed. Clearing a data series or data format from a chart is a quick and easy process.

Clearing a Data Series or Format

1 Select the data series you want to modify, and press **Delete**.

2 Select **S**eries to delete the selected data series, or select **F**ormats to clear only the data format.

3 Select **OK**.

DELETING AN EMBEDDED CHART

Why Delete a Chart

As your worksheets evolve, you may no longer need to chart certain blocks of data. Having extraneous charts cluttering up your worksheet not only wastes worksheet space, but also makes the worksheet harder to understand. To keep your worksheets concise, you should delete old charts as soon as they're no longer needed.

Deleting an Embedded Chart

1 Click on the chart you want to delete.

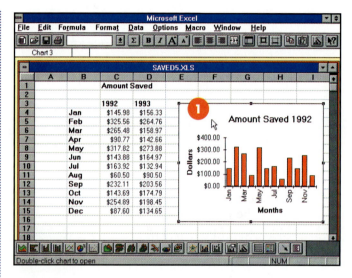

2 Press **Delete**.

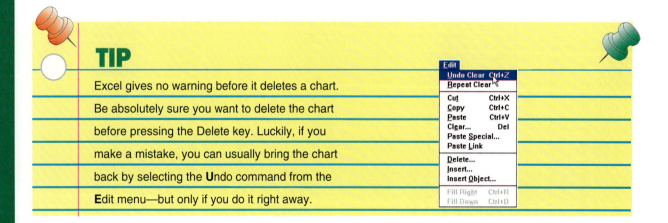

TIP

Excel gives no warning before it deletes a chart. Be absolutely sure you want to delete the chart before pressing the Delete key. Luckily, if you make a mistake, you can usually bring the chart back by selecting the **U**ndo command from the **E**dit menu—but only if you do it right away.

96

PART 5

Printing a Worksheet

This part describes various ways to print your worksheets, something you might want to do for several reasons. You might, for example, want to use a printed copy of a worksheet in a presentation, or maybe you need "hard copy" you can refer to without starting your computer. When you have finished this part, you will be able to select a printer, set up pages, use print preview, print all or part of a worksheet, and add headers and footers to your worksheets.

- Selecting a Printer
- Printing an Entire Worksheet
- Printing Part of a Worksheet
- Using Print Preview
- Setting Up Pages
- Using Page Breaks
- Printing Row or Column Titles
- Adding Headers and Footers

SELECTING A PRINTER

Why Select a Printer?

Before printing a worksheet, you must tell Excel what printer to use. If your system has only one printer connected to it, that printer is probably already selected for you. However, it's still a good idea to check before attempting to print a worksheet. Otherwise, you could waste a lot of time and paper. You can select a printer easily using the File menu's Page Setup command.

Selecting a Printer

1 Select Page Setup from the File menu.

2 Select the Printer Setup button.

3 Select the printer you want to use.

4 Select **OK**, or press **Enter**.

5 Select **OK**, or press **Enter**.

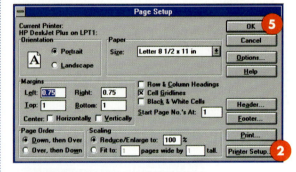

98

PRINTING AN ENTIRE WORKSHEET

The Easiest Way to Print

The easiest way to print a worksheet is to print the entire sheet and let Excel worry about fitting it on the pages. If your worksheet is small, it can probably fit on one page. If your worksheet is too large to fit on a single page, Excel divides the worksheet into page-sized pieces, both vertically and horizontally. Excel then prints each piece on its own page, after which you can assemble the pieces with scissors and tape.

TIP

You can force the worksheet to fit on a certain number of pages by manipulating the settings in the Page Setup dialog box. Select the Page **S**etup from the Print dialog box after step 2, then change the Scaling to fit to a certain number of pages. This option adjusts the font size of the printout until it fits on the specified number of pages.

Select this button... ... then indicate the number of pages to fit to.

TIP

You can avoid the Print dialog box by clicking on the toolbar's **Print** button. Excel then immediately starts printing the entire document.

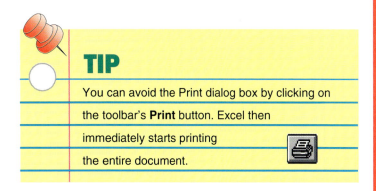

PRINTING AN ENTIRE WORKSHEET

Printing an Entire Worksheet

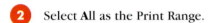 Select **P**rint from the **F**ile menu, or press **Ctrl+Shift+F12**.

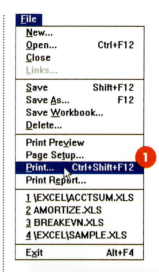

 Select **A**ll as the Print Range.

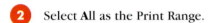 Select **OK**, or press **Enter**.

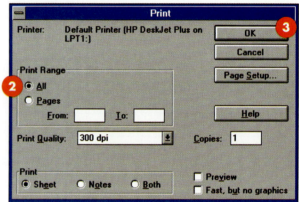

PRINTING PART OF A WORKSHEET

Why Print Part of a Worksheet?

Often, you need to print only a small portion of your worksheet. For example, suppose you have a worksheet containing sales records for a group of employees, with each employee having her own table. When you're interested in printing the record for a specific employee, there's no point in printing the entire worksheet. Simply set the print area to only the table you need.

LEARNING THE LINGO

Print area: When you want to print only a section of a worksheet, you select a print area. The print area stays in effect until you remove it.

Select All button: The blank button at the intersection of the column letter row and the row numbers column.

Printing Part of a Worksheet

1 Select the range that you want to print.

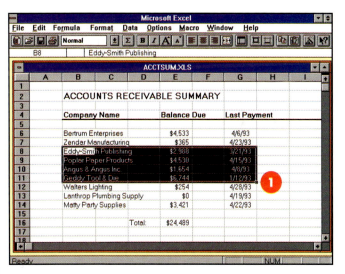

2 Select Set Print Area from the Options menu.

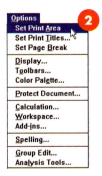

101

PRINTING PART OF A WORKSHEET

3 Select **P**rint from the **F**ile menu, or press **Ctrl+Shift+F12**.

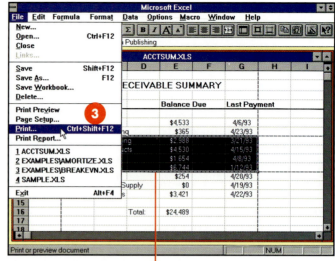

Print area is outlined on the screen.

4 Select **OK**, or press **Enter**.

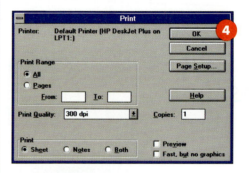

5 Click on the **Select All** button, or press **Ctrl+Shift+Spacebar**.

6 Select Remove Print **A**rea from the **O**ptions menu.

102

USING PRINT PREVIEW

Why Use Print Preview?

There's nothing quite so frustrating as printing a document only to discover that it didn't come out the way you expected. Experimenting with layouts by printing documents is time consuming, expensive, and wastes paper. So, before printing a document, make it a habit to check the layout with Print Preview.

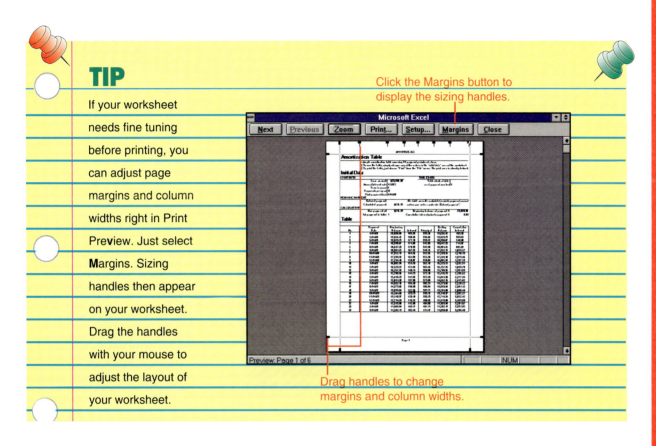

TIP

If your worksheet needs fine tuning before printing, you can adjust page margins and column widths right in Print Preview. Just select **Ma**rgins. Sizing handles then appear on your worksheet. Drag the handles with your mouse to adjust the layout of your worksheet.

Click the Margins button to display the sizing handles.

Drag handles to change margins and column widths.

Printing a Worksheet

103

USING PRINT PREVIEW

Using Print Preview

1. Select Print Preview from the File menu.

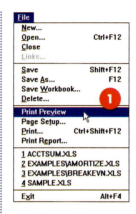

2. (Optional) To see the next page of your worksheet, select **N**ext.

3. (Optional) To see a previous page of your worksheet, select **P**revious.

4. (Optional) To see part of the worksheet in greater detail, select **Z**oom, or click the magnifying-glass cursor on the worksheet.

5. (Optional) To print the worksheet from Print Preview, select Prin**t**.

6. When you're finished, select Close.

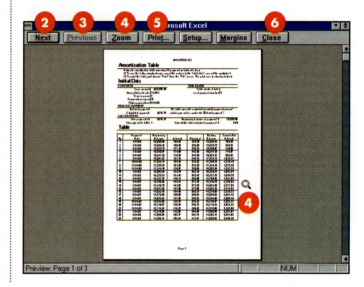

SETTING UP PAGES

Why Create Page Setups?

While printing a worksheet with the default page setup is the easiest way to get your data on paper, if you have special needs, you can modify the page setup any way you like. Using Excel's Page Setup dialog box, you can change page orientation, paper size, margins, scaling, and other options that control how your finished printout looks.

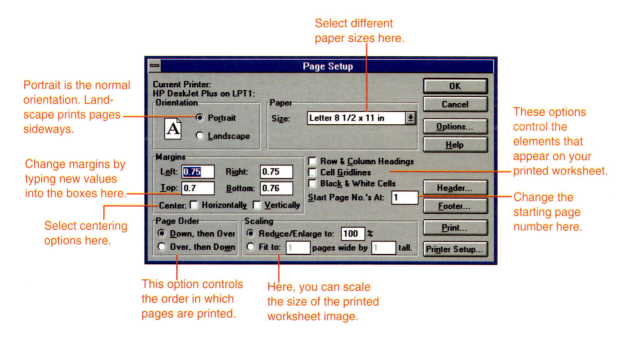

Select different paper sizes here.

Portrait is the normal orientation. Landscape prints pages sideways.

Change margins by typing new values into the boxes here.

Select centering options here.

This option controls the order in which pages are printed.

Here, you can scale the size of the printed worksheet image.

These options control the elements that appear on your printed worksheet.

Change the starting page number here.

LEARNING THE LINGO

Scaling: Scaling means to reduce or enlarge the size of your worksheet's image. For example, to print a worksheet at half its normal size, you'd reduce it by 50%. To print your worksheet twice as large, you'd enlarge it by 200%.

SETTING UP PAGES

Setting Up Pages

1. Select Page Setup from the File menu.

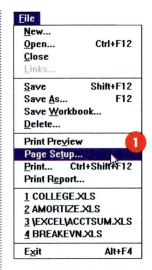

2. Change the page setup options you need to change, and then select **OK**, or press **Enter**.

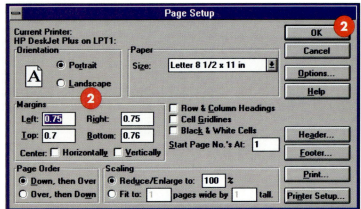

TIP

The Page Setup dialog box varies slightly depending on the current document. For example, in the Page Setup dialog box for a Chart document, some options are unavailable. On the other hand, a new Chart Size option is available.

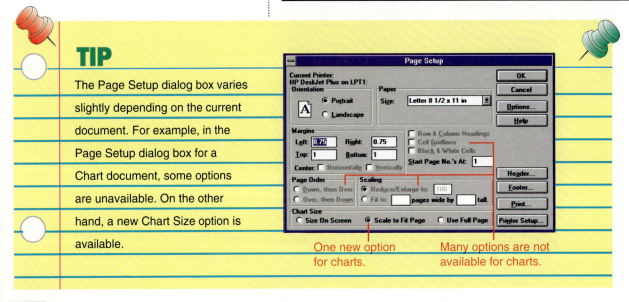

One new option for charts.

Many options are not available for charts.

USING PAGE BREAKS

Why Insert Page Breaks?

If you want sections of a worksheet to appear on specific pages, you can move those sections to new columns and rows in order to make them appear on the page you want. However, an easier way to place a worksheet section on its own page is to insert page breaks into the document. When Excel is printing a document and sees a page break, it automatically ejects the current page from the printer and starts a new one.

When you set a page break, Excel places a break to the left of the current cell and a break above the current cell. Other pages in the document are readjusted to reflect the new page layout.

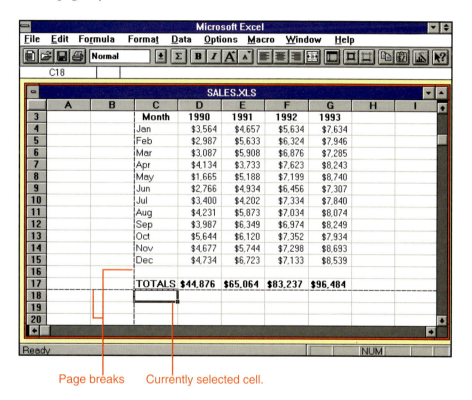

Page breaks   Currently selected cell.

LEARNING THE LINGO

Page break: A page break is a marker that tells Excel where to eject the current page from the printer and start a new one. Excel automatically places page breaks to divide a worksheet into page-sized pieces. However, you can add your own page breaks and so force Excel to organize the printout the way you want it to be organized.

USING PAGE BREAKS

Inserting Page Breaks

1 Move to the cell where you want the page break inserted.

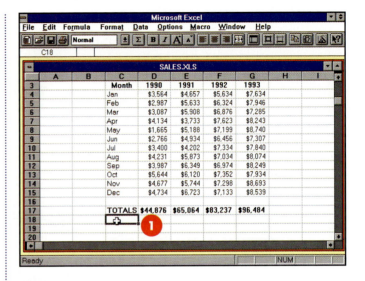

2 Select Set Page **B**reak from the **O**ptions menu.

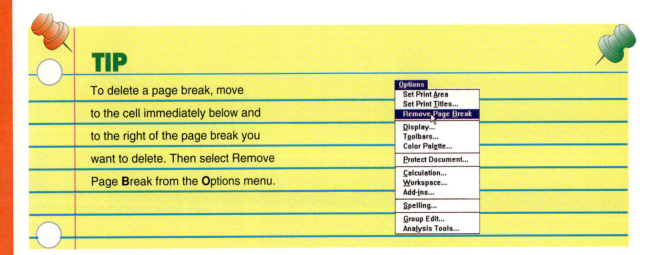

TIP

To delete a page break, move to the cell immediately below and to the right of the page break you want to delete. Then select Remove Page **B**reak from the **O**ptions menu.

108

USING PAGE BREAKS

Exercise

Load the worksheet and chart named **SAVED4.XLS** that you created in an earlier exercise. Then insert a page break, as shown in the figure, so that the worksheet and chart will print on separate pages.

1 Move to cell **E1** (or if your chart is positioned differently, to the first row of the column in which your chart begins).

2 Select Set Page **B**reak from the **O**ptions menu.

3 Use Print Preview to see that the table and chart are actually on separate pages.

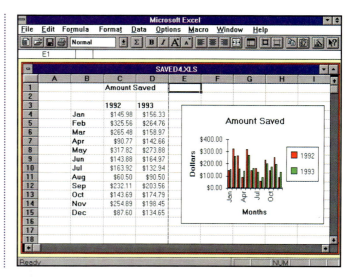

TIP

Your worksheets can have two kinds of page breaks. *Automatic page breaks* are included automatically by Excel, based on the settings in the Page Setup dialog box. *Manual page breaks* are the ones you add with the Set Page **B**reak command. How can you tell them apart? In an automatic page break, the dashes that make up the page-break line are farther apart than those in a manual page break.

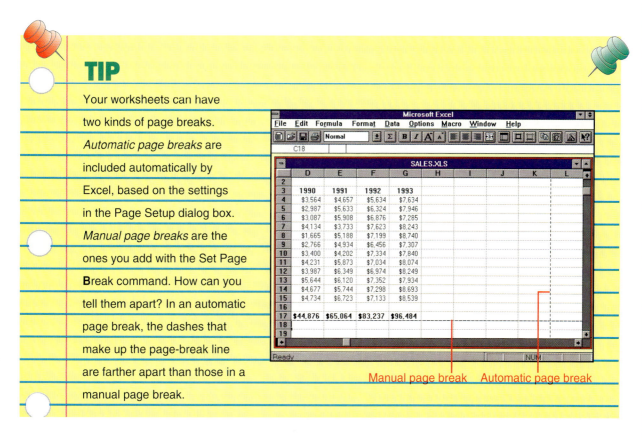

Manual page break   Automatic page break

109

PRINTING ROW OR COLUMN TITLES

Why Print Titles?

In large worksheets, tables of data may get split among multiple pages, making it hard to determine which data goes with what row and column labels. Fortunately, Excel enables you to specify row or column titles to be printed on every page. That way, no matter how many pages of data you have, each page appears with clearly marked columns and rows.

Printing Row or Column Titles

1. Select the row or column that contains the titles you want to use.

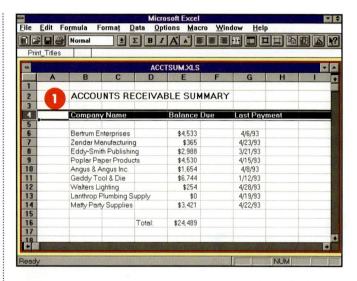

2. Select Set Print Titles from the Options menu.

3. Select OK, or press Enter.

110

PRINTING ROW OR COLUMN TITLES

Exercise

Load the worksheet and chart named **SAVED4.XLS** that you created in an earlier exercise. Then specify the table's column titles as row print titles.

1 Select row 3.

2 Select Set Print **T**itles from the **O**ptions menu.

3 Select **OK**, or press **Enter**.

4 Set a page break at row 10, and then go to Page Preview to see that the row titles appear on every page.

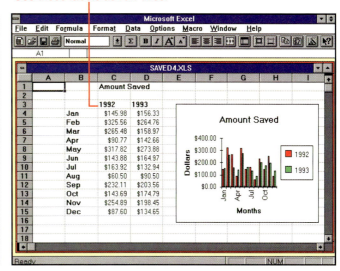

Use these labels as row titles.

QUICK REFRESHER

To select a row or column, click on its row number or column letter, or press **Shift+Spacebar** (for the row) or **Ctrl+Spacebar** (for the column).

TIP

To remove titles, select Set Print **T**itles from the **O**ptions menu, use the keyboard's **Backspace** key to clear the text from the Print Titles boxes, and then select **OK**, or press **Enter**.

QUICK REFRESHER

To set a page break, choose Set Page **B**reak from the **O**ptions menu. To use Print Preview, select Print Pre**v**iew from the **F**ile menu.

111

ADDING HEADERS AND FOOTERS

Why Use Headers and Footers?

Headers and footers allow you to print page numbers, file descriptions, and other information on every page of a printout. Headers are printed at the top of the page, and footers are printed at the bottom. To help you construct headers and footers, Excel includes special codes that represent page numbers, date and time stamps, and file names in your headers and footers. In addition, you can specify font types and sizes.

The Header and Footer dialog box lets you specify which header elements to print at three positions: left, center, and right. Any text you type in a section appears as part of the header. In addition, the dialog box's buttons give you quick access to the codes you need to add pages numbers, dates, and other common header and footer elements.

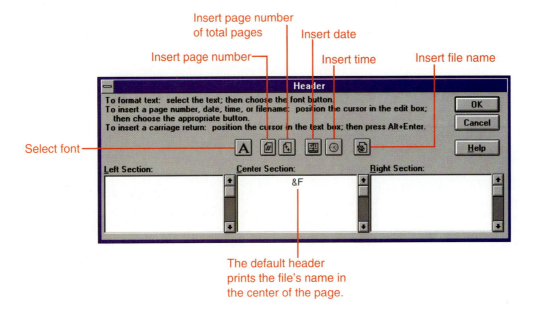

ADDING HEADERS AND FOOTERS

Adding Header and Footers

1 Select Page Setup from the File menu.

2 Select the Header or Footer button.

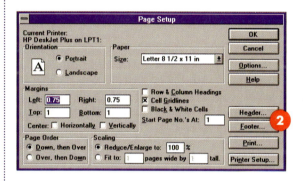

3 Follow the instructions in the Header or Footer dialog box to create your header or footer, and then select **OK**.

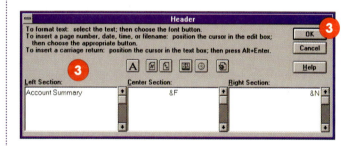

4 Select **OK**, or press **Enter**.

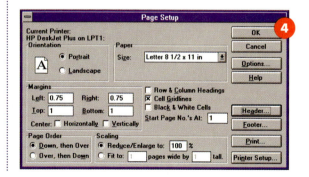

113

ADDING HEADERS AND FOOTERS

Exercise

Load the sample worksheet **COLLEGE.XLS** from Excel's **EXAMPLES** directory, and then add the header shown in the figure.

1 Select Page Setup from the File menu.

2 Select Header.

3 In the Left Section box, type **College Expenses**.

4 Click in the Right Section box to move the cursor there.

5 Click on the date button, type a space, and then click on the time button.

6 Select OK.

7 Select OK.

8 Go to Print Preview to see the header you created.

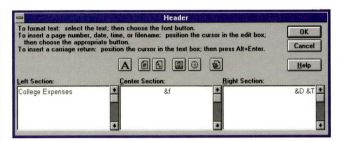

TIP

You create headers and footers in exactly the same way. The only difference is where they're printed on the page.

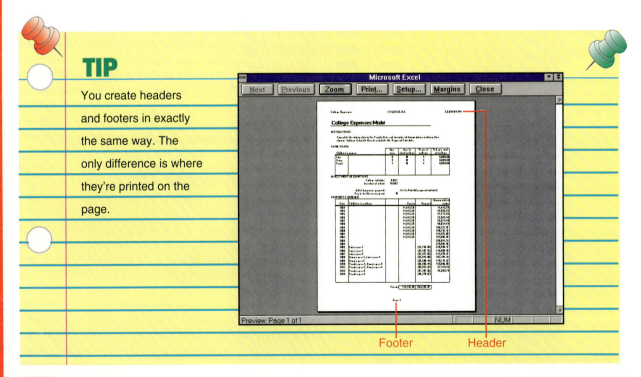

114

Installing Excel

When you first open Excel's package, you'll find that the program is shipped on five high-density floppy disks. Before you can use Excel, you must install it onto your computer. In most cases, installation is automatic, with your needing to do little more than answer a few questions and swap disks when prompted. Although Excel offers a custom installation that lets you select what portions of the program to install, unless you're sure of what you're doing, you should use the automated installation described here.

The installation instructions here assume you'll install Excel from drive A. If you need to use drive B, just substitute B for A in the instructions.

QUICK REFRESHER

If you have a mouse, you'll want to use it for the installation. The skills you'll need are:

- **Point:** To move the mouse on its pad until the on-screen pointer points at the desired object.
- **Click:** To press and release the left mouse button once. When you "click on" an object, you first point to it and then click.
- **Double-click:** To press and release the left mouse button twice quickly.

QUICK REFRESHER

If you're a keyboard-only user, you'll need to use some key combinations to complete the installation. When you see two keys written with a plus sign between them, such as **Alt+C**, it means you should hold down the first key and then press the second key.

Installing Excel

1 Start your computer, and type **WIN** to run Windows.

2 Insert Excel's disk #1 into drive A.

3 If you don't see the Program Manager window, double-click on the icon labelled **Program Manager** to open it.

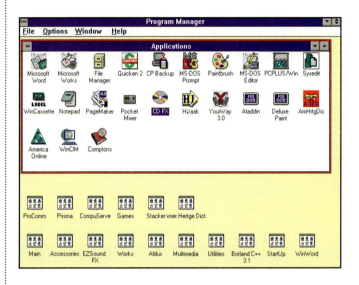

4 Click on **File** at the top left corner of the screen, or hold down the **Alt** key, and press **F**.

5 Click on the **R**un command, or press **R**.

6 Type **a:setup**, and press **Enter**.

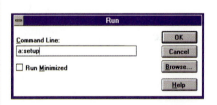

7 If you want to install Excel on drive C:, click on **Continue**, or press **Alt+C**. Otherwise, type the drive and directory in the Install to box before selecting **C**ontinue.

8 Click on **Yes**, or press **Alt+Y**.

9 Click on the **Complete Installation** button, or press **Enter**.

10 Click on the **No** button, or press **Enter**.

11 Click on the **Update** button, or press **Enter**.

12 Place the requested disk into drive A, and press **Enter**.

13 Repeat step 12 until Excel is fully installed.

14 Click on **OK**, or press **Enter**.

Glossary

Alignment   Alignment is the way data is positioned within a cell.

Arguments   The values functions need in order to calculate a result. A function's arguments are enclosed in parentheses.

Attached Text   Text that is connected to a particular chart element.

Axis   A chart has two axes: the Y axis usually displays data values, and the X axis usually displays data categories.

Cell   A cell is a small box at the intersection of a row and column in the worksheet. Each cell can hold a single piece of data or a formula.

Cell cursor   The cell cursor is a dark box that surrounds the current cell.

Cell format   A cell's format is the way a cell displays its data, including the number type, the alignment of data within the cell, and text styles, such as bold or italics.

Cell range   A cell range refers to a block of cells and consists of two cell references separated by a colon.

Cell reference   A column letter followed by a row number that refers to the value in a particular cell.

Chart document   A chart document is not part of a worksheet and has its own window.

Check marks   A check mark next to a menu option means the option is currently selected.

Click   Press and release the left mouse button.

Column   A column is a vertical line of cells, each identified by a letter.

Command button   An on-screen button object that you can click to select a specific Excel command.

Data marker   A data marker represents a value in a chart. For example, in a bar chart, the data markers are the bars, whereas in a pie chart, the data markers are the pie slices.

Data series   A data series in a chart is equivalent to a column of data in a worksheet. For example, a chart created from a two-column table will usually have two data series, each plotted with its own color.

Directory   Directories are like little file cabinets on your hard drive that help you organize your files. They can contain either files or other directories.

Double-click   Press and release the left mouse button twice quickly.

GLOSSARY

Drag   Point to a screen object and then hold down the left mouse button while you move the mouse, dragging the pointer across the screen.

Ellipsis   An ellipsis is three dots (...). When an ellipsis follows a menu command, the command displays a dialog box when selected.

Embedded chart   An embedded chart is part of a worksheet.

File   Your worksheets are stored on your hard disk in a *file*, a collection of related data stored as a single unit.

Font   A set of characters, all of which belong to the same design family.

Grayed-out   Grayed-out menu commands are displayed lighter than other commands and cannot be selected.

Hot keys   Keystrokes you can use to instantly select a menu command.

Insertion cursor   A blinking vertical bar that shows where the next typed character will appear.

Label   A series of characters that have no numerical value. A label is usually used for headings and notations.

Legend   A chart legend tells you what the different parts of a chart mean.

Minimized   Shrunken to the size of an icon; windows that are not in use are often minimized so they do not clutter the screen.

Operator precedence   The order in which arithmetic operations are performed, also called "order of operations."

Operators   Excel supports many operators that you can use in your formulas, including addition (+), subtraction (-), multiplication (*), division (/), and percentage (%).

Orientation   Orientation is the direction in which the characters of the text are displayed.

Page break   A page break is a marker that tells Excel where to eject the current page from the printer and start a new one. Excel automatically places page breaks to divide a worksheet into page-sized pieces. However, you can add your own page breaks and so force Excel to organize the printout the way you want it to be organized.

GLOSSARY

Point   Position the mouse pointer over an object on the screen.

Print area   When you want to print only a section of a worksheet, you select a print area. The print area stays in effect until you remove it.

Program icon   A small picture representing a program you can run. The program name usually appears under the picture.

Program group   A window containing one or more program icons.

Program group icon   A small picture representing a program group that has been minimized.

Row   A row is a horizontal line of cells, each identified by a number.

Scaling   Scaling means to reduce or enlarge the size of your worksheet's image. For example, to print a worksheet at half its normal size, you'd reduce it by 50%. To print your worksheet twice as large, you'd enlarge it by 200%.

Select All button   The blank button at the intersection of the column letter row and the row numbers column.

Selection letter   The underlined letter in a menu or command name.

Status Bar   An area at the bottom of Excel's main window that displays messages about the worksheet's status.

Text Styles   Attributes such as bold, italic, and underlining that can be applied to text.

Toggle   To switch an option from on to off or from off to on.

Toolbar   A stationary row of command buttons at the top or bottom of Excel's main window.

Toolbox   A small, movable box containing command buttons.

Unattached Text   Text that sits on top of the chart, unconnected to a particular element.

Worksheet functions   These are built-in functions that you can use to calculate values. Some functions are SUM, which calculates sums; AVERAGE, which calculates averages; and SQRT, which calculates square roots. There are hundreds of worksheet functions, all of which are listed in the *Function Reference* that came with your copy of Excel.

Index

Symbols

- (subtraction) operator, 46
\# (pound sign) in cells, 75
' (single quote), 41, 43
* (multiplication) operator, 46
+ (addition) operator, 46
/ (division) operator, 46
= (equals sign), 47
^ (exponentiation) operator, 46
... (ellipsis), 14, 120

A-B

absolute references, 58
active window, 30
addition (+) operator, 46
alignment, 73-74, 119
alphanumeric keys, 8
arguments, 52, 119
arrow keys, 8
attached text, 119
attributes, 77-78
automatic page breaks, 109
axes, 119

blocks of cells, *see* ranges
bold text, 77-78

C

cell cursor, 2-3, 38, 119
cells, 2-3, 119
    aligning data, 73-74
    changing widths, 75-76
    clearing, 65-66
    copying, 58-60
    editing contents, 56-57
    formats, 65, 119
    moving, 58-60
    ranges, *see* ranges
    references, 3, 48-50, 119
    replacing data, 68
    searching for data, 67
    selecting, 38-39
    sorting data, 69-71
center-aligned data, 73
chart documents, 86-87, 119
charts
    clearing data series/formats, 95
    creating, 80-83
    deleting elements, 94
    editing, 88-89
    embedded, *see* embedded charts
    legends, adding, 92-93
    types, changing, 84-85
    values, changing, 90-91
ChartWizard, 80-83, 88-89
check boxes, 20-21
check marks by commands, 14, 119
clearing
    cells, 65-66
    chart data series/formats, 95
clicking, 9, 13, 119
closing
    dialog boxes without selecting items, 15, 20
    menus without selecting items, 15
    worksheets, 30

columns, 2, 119
    changing widths, 75-76
    deleting, 63-64
    inserting, 61-62
    selecting, 38
    sorting, 71
    titles, 110-111
command buttons, 20-23, 119
commands
    ... (ellipsis), 14, 120
    Alignment (Format menu), 74
    check marks by, 14, 119
    Clear (Edit menu), 66
    Close (File menu), 30
    Column Width (Format menu), 76
    Contents (Help menu), 24-25
    Delete
        Edit menu, 64
        File menu, 35
    Exit (File menu), 36
    Find (Formula menu), 67
    Font (Format menu), 78
    grayed-out, 14, 120
    Insert (Edit menu), 61-62
    New (File menu), 29
    Number (Format menu), 72
    Open (File menu), 27-28
    Page Setup (File menu), 98, 106, 113-114
    Paste Function (Formula menu), 53-54
    Print (File menu), 100, 102
    Print Preview (File menu), 104
    Remove Page Break (Options menu), 108
    Remove Print Area (Options menu), 102
    Replace (Formula menu), 68
    Run (Windows File menu), 116
    Save (File menu), 32
    Save As (File menu), 33-34
    Search (Help menu), 26
    selecting, 14-16
        from Toolbars or Toolboxes, 22
    selection letters, 5, 14, 121
    Set Page Break (Options menu), 108-109
    Set Print Area (Options menu), 101
    Set Print Titles (Options menu), 110-111
    Shortcut menu, 65
    Sort (Data menu), 69-71
    Toolbars (Options menu), 23
    Undo (Edit menu), 96
    WIN, 12
    worksheet-name (Window menu), 31
    Workspace (Options menu), 58
computer components, 7-10
control-menu box, 17-20, 30
copying cells, 58-60
CPUs (central processing units), 8
cursors
    cell, 2-3, 38, 119
    insertion, 57, 120
    magnifying-glass, 104

D

data, 2-3
    alignment, 73-74
        default, 42
    replacing, 68
    searching for, 67
    sorting, 69-71
data markers, 91, 119
data series, 92, 119
    clearing, 95
dates
    entering, 44-45
    in headers and footers, 112

Delete key, 66
deleting
    chart elements, 94
    columns and rows, 63-64
    embedded charts, 96
    page breaks, 108
    row/column titles, 111
    worksheets, 35
dialog boxes, 15, 20-21
directories, 10, 28, 119
disk drives, 8, 10
disks, 8, 10
division (/) operator, 46
documents, 1
    chart, 119
        changing embedded charts to, 86-87
DOS prompt, 12
double-clicking, 9, 13, 119
dragging, 20, 39, 120
drop-down list boxes, 20-21

E

editing
    cell contents, 56-57
    charts, 88-89
ellipsis (...), 14, 120
embedded charts, 120
    changing to chart documents, 86-87
    deleting, 96
equals sign (=), 47
Excel
    exiting, 17, 36
    features, 1-2
    installing, 115-117
    starting, 12-13
exponentiation (^) operator, 46

F

files, 9-10, 28, 120
    extensions, 33
    names in headers and footers, 112
finding data in cells, 67
floppy disk drives, 10
floppy disks, 10
fonts, 77-78, 120
    in headers and footers, 112
footers, 112-114
formats
    cells, 65, 119
    charts, clearing, 95
    dates and times, 44-45
    numbers, changing, 72
formatting, 3
    aligning data in cells, 73-74
    column widths, 75-76
    fonts and text attributes, 77-78
    headers and footers, 112-114
    page breaks, 107-109
    setting up pages, 105-106
formula bar, 2, 40
formulas, 2-3
    cell ranges in, 51
    cell references in, 49-50
    entering, 46-48
    functions in, 52-54
function keys, 8
functions, 46, 48, 52-54, 121

G-H

grayed-out commands, 14, 120

handles, chart elements, 94
hard disks, 10
headers, 112-114
Help, 24-26
hot keys, 14, 120

I-J

icons
    Microsoft Excel, 13
    program, 13, 121
    program group, 12-13, 121
    Program Manager, 116
inactive windows, 30
insertion cursor, 57, 120
installing Excel, 115-117
italic text, 77-78

jump terms, 24

K-L

keyboard shortcuts
    Clear (Del), 66
    Close (Ctrl+F4), 31
    Control menu
        main window (Alt+Spacebar), 18
        worksheet window (Alt+hyphen), 18
    Copy (Ctrl+C), 60
    Cut (Ctrl+X), 60
    Exit (Alt+F4), 36
    Find (Shift+F5), 67
    Formula bar (F2), 57
    hot keys, 14, 120
    Open (Ctrl+F12), 27
    Print (Ctrl+Shift+F12), 100
    Save (Shift+F12), 32
    Save As (F12), 34
    Select All (Ctrl+Shift+Spacebar), 38, 102
    Select block of cells (Shift+arrow key), 38
    Select column (Ctrl+Spacebar), 38
    Select row (Shift+Spacebar), 38
    Shortcut menu (Shift+F10), 65
    Undo (Ctrl+Z), 96
keyboards, 7-8

labels, 40-41, 120
landscape orientation, 105
leading zeros, 43
left-aligned data, 73
legends, 82, 92-93, 120
list boxes, 20-21

M

magnifying-glass cursor, 104
manual page breaks, 109
margins, changing, 103, 105
Maximize button, 17-19
menus, 14-16
Minimize button, 17-19
minimized windows, 13, 120
monitors, 7
mouse, 7, 9
mouse pointer, dragging, 39
moving
    cells, 58-60
    dialog boxes, 20
    windows, 18
multiplication (*) operator, 46

N-O

numbering pages in headers and footers, 112
number formats, changing, 72

opening
    Toolbars or Toolboxes, 23
    worksheets, 27-28
operator precedence, 46, 48, 120
operators, 48, 120
option buttons, 20-21
orientation, 73, 105, 120

P-Q

page breaks, 107-109, 120
pages
    numbering in headers and footers, 112
    setting up, 105-106
paper sizes, 105
pointing, 9, 13, 121
portrait orientation, 105
ports, 8
pound sign (#) in cells, 75
previewing worksheets, 103-104
print areas, 101, 121
printers, selecting, 98
printing
    row/column titles, 110-111
    worksheets, 99-102
program group icons, 12-13, 121
program groups, 13, 121
program icons, 13, 121
programs
    Setup, 116-117
    spreadsheet, 1

R

RAM (random-access memory), 8
ranges, 119
    copying or moving, 58-60
    in formulas, 51
    selecting, 38-39
references, cells, 3, 48-50, 58, 119
relative references, 58
replacing data in cells, 68
Restore button, 17-19
restoring deleted charts, 96
right-aligned data, 73
right-clicking, 9
rows, 2, 121
    deleting, 63-64
    inserting, 61-62
    selecting, 38
    titles, 110-111

S

saving worksheets, 32-34
scaling, 105, 121
scroll arrows, 17-19
scroll bars, 17-19
scroll box, 17-19
Select All button, 38, 101-102, 121
selection letters, 5, 14, 121
Setup program, 116-117
Shortcut menu, 65
single quote ('), 41, 43
sorting data in cells, 69-71

spreadsheet programs, 1
spreadsheets, *see* worksheets
starting Excel, 12-13
status bar, 57, 121
subdirectories, 10
subtraction (–) operator, 46
system units, 7-8

T

text, 2-3
    attached, 119
    fonts and attributes, 77-78
    unattached, 121
text boxes, 20-21
text styles, 77, 121
times
    entering, 44-45
    in headers and footers, 112
title bar, 17-20
titles, row/column, 110-111
toggling, 20, 121
Toolbars, 22-23, 121
    alignment tools, 73
    Bold text tool, 77
    chart-type tools, 84
    ChartWizard tool, 80
    font size tools, 77
    Help tool, 26
    Italic text tool, 77
    New Document tool, 29
    Open tool, 28
    Print tool, 99
    Save tool, 29, 32
Toolboxes, 22-23, 121

U-V

unattached text, 121
underlined text, 77-78
undoing last action, 96

values, 2-3
    entering, 42-43
    in charts, changing, 90-91

W-Z

windows
    active, 30
    components, 17
    controlling, 17
    creating for charts, 86-87
    inactive, 30
    minimized, 13, 120
worksheet functions, 46, 48, 52-54, 121
worksheets
    closing, 30-31
    creating, 29
    deleting, 35
    opening, 27-28
    previewing, 103-104
    printing, 99-102
    saving, 32-34
    selecting, 38
    setting up pages, 105-106

zeros, leading, 43
zooming worksheets, 104